THE PRINCIPLES OF WEALTH

Timeless Rules and Habits for Greater Prosperity

KELVIN WONG

The Principles of Wealth: Timeless Rules and Habits for Greater Prosperity
First edition. January 28, 2019.
Second edition. August 18, 2021.

International Edition
Business & Money / Personal Finance / Wealth Management
www.kelvinwong.com

Copyright © 2019, 2021 by Kelvin Wong.
All rights reserved. No part of this publication may be reproduced, stored in a retrieval system or transmitted, in any form or by any means, electronic, mechanical, photocopying, recording or otherwise, without the prior permission of the copyright owner.

ISBN-10: 1798278731
ISBN-13: 978-1-79827-873-4

Disclaimer:

This publication contains the opinions and ideas of its author. It aims to provide readers with a general overview of personal finance and wealth building. The book is sold with the understanding that neither the author nor the publisher is engaged in rendering legal, tax, financial, investment, real estate, accounting, insurance, or other professional advice or services by publishing this book. The strategies outlined in this book may not be suitable for every individual, and are not guaranteed or warranted to produce any particular results. Readers are cautioned to rely on their own judgment and act appropriately. As each individual situation is unique, questions relevant to personal finances and specific to the individual should be addressed to a competent professional.

While every precaution has been taken in the preparation of this book, the author and publisher assume no responsibility for errors, omissions, accuracy or completeness of the information contained herein. The author and publisher specifically disclaim any liability, loss, or risk that is incurred as a consequence, directly or indirectly, of the use and application of any contents of this work. Some names and identifying details have been changed to protect the privacy of individuals.

DEDICATION

I dedicate this book to my lovely wife, Amelia, who is a perfect partner to me and a great mother to our children. She has always been managing her finances in a generous and moral manner, and is a great example of someone who adhere to the principles of wealth.

And to my wonderful sons, Joshua and Isaac, who have endured my countless long lectures about money. I hope that both of you will always get ahead financially in the years to come.

Last but not least, this book is dedicated to you, the reader, who is the motivation and reason for me writing this book. I wish you massive success in your quest for greater prosperity!

CONTENTS

	Introduction	1
	PART ONE: THINK RICH	5
1	The Meaning of Wealth	7
2	Wrong Money Beliefs	15
3	Why Are Most People Not Rich?	22
4	It's All in the Mind	29
5	Attitudes and Habits That Will Make You Rich	36
6	Complaining Won't Make Things Better	42
7	Value Your Greatest Asset	51
8	Dare to Dream Again	57
	PART TWO: GET RICH	63
9	Where Are You Financially?	65
10	Invest in Yourself	69
11	Create a Budget	77
12	Keep a Part of All You Earn	81
13	Avoid the Debt Trap	88
14	Save to Invest	95
15	The Power of Compounding	102

16	Take Calculated Risks	107
17	Develop Other Income Streams	114
	PART THREE: STAY RICH	124
18	Live a Frugal Life	126
19	The Price of Ego	136
20	Stop Spending Money You Don't Have	141
21	Invest to Beat Inflation	148
22	Use the 80/20 Rule to Manage More Efficiently	155
23	Get Rich Quick and Go Broke Fast	159
24	Health is Wealth	167
	PART FOUR: SHARE YOUR RICHES	177
25	Be a Blessing to Others	179
26	Don't Be a Money Lender	185
27	Tough Love Breeds Smart Children	191
28	Enough Is Enough	198
	Conclusion	205

Prosperity is inevitable for those who understand the principles of wealth and live by them.
—Kelvin Wong

Introduction

Do you want to be wealthy? Honestly, who doesn't? It is hard to find someone who doesn't care about money, especially in these turbulent economic times the world is facing today. The reason you're reading this book means you wish to find ways to build wealth. Well, you have come to the right place!

Save for the few who are born into wealthy families, most of us have to work hard to earn a living. We have to work even harder to save some money for investment to create wealth. It is the dream of many to become rich one day and living a life that is free from worrying about money. We all wish to be well-off, and we admire others who already are. We wonder how they become wealthy, and want to know how we can do it too.

Let me start by saying that *The Principles of Wealth* is not one of those "how to get rich quick" books. This book isn't written for people looking for quick and easy ways to get wealthy. Rather, this book speaks about the timeless rules of wealth building, success habits of wealthy people, as well as money management strategies that remain relevant in any economy. There are many books out there telling you how to get rich quickly. These books generally include some basic strategies based on future forecasts and projections. However, the success of the strategies revealed in those books are dependent on certain economic conditions.

Therein lies the problem—the world economic situation changes, and no country's economy remain steady all the time. No one living on earth can predict the future. Only God knows the future.

There are also many get-rich-quick schemes offering you an easy path to wealth. Believe me, these get-rich-quick schemes work. Wait a minute, I hear you protesting already. Or maybe even crying! Let me repeat: get-rich-quick schemes do work, just not for you. They work for those people who launch such deceitful schemes. Why is that so? Because the world is full of gullible, greedy and lazy people seeking instant wealth. And such schemes meet their instant gratification needs perfectly! There is really no such thing as easy money. Most investments promising minimal capital or efforts to get rich quickly are scams. If you are presented with any propositions of fast and easy money that sound too good to be true, they probably are. Now, remember this important truth again—there are no get-rich-quick schemes available in this world that can work for you!

We must always remind ourselves that things don't come easy, especially money. Please don't expect money to fall from the sky. You need to work hard and put in the necessary efforts to get the things you want. I know. Because I am sharing from my personal experience. I'm a living example of someone who has managed to turn his financial destiny around. I started off life being poor but went on to become a multimillionaire.

How did an ordinary guy like me achieve that?

To begin with, I wasn't born with a silver spoon in my mouth. And I certainly didn't inherit millions of dollars. Neither did I strike lottery or won big at the casino. In fact, not once in my life had I gambled, and I don't plan to do so in the future. I started my journey towards financial freedom and wealth creation by taking the first step to develop my financial literacy. I bought and read hundreds of books on personal finance, and then applied what I have learned by taking actionable steps to improve my financial health.

Over the years, I live a simple and frugal life—spending less than I earn, saving a portion of my income regularly, and investing my savings to grow my wealth. While working as an employee to earn my salary, I stay invested to let my money work for me at the same time. Eventually in 2007, I joined those in the "Millionaire Club" when my net worth (my total assets minus my total liabilities but excluding the market value of the house that I'm living in) finally exceeded US$1 million. I then decided to quit corporate employment the same year to manage and grow my investment portfolio full-time. Despite being a millionaire for many years already, my lifestyle hasn't changed much. I am still living frugally today. The key to financial success is to invest money to accumulate income-generating assets instead of spending most of your money on liabilities. This is how an ordinary person like me can achieve extraordinary wealth. It's not rocket science. And if I can do it, you can too!

The Principles of Wealth contains much of the wisdom needed for you to amass a substantial fortune. It provides wealth principles, money rules, success habits and strategies for you to understand, and to take action to achieve wealth. I'm assuming you want to be rich (the legal way), are willing to get rid of bad money habits, and are ready to put in the effort and hard work to achieve your dream. You won't be getting rich quickly, but the odds of you making some serious money will greatly increase. You will become a richer and happier person if you adhere to the wealth rules reveal in this book. That, I can assure you.

As the saying goes, "Give a man a fish, and you feed him for a day. Teach a man to fish, and you feed him for a lifetime." In the same spirit, I'll be teaching you how to fish instead of providing you with the fish. I took the no-bull, no-nonsense and straight-talking approach in writing this book. Timeless rules of wealth and the habits of the rich are revealed. These principles are crucial for achieving financial success. I'll also be sharing money management ideas that are not only relevant today, but applicable for the future economy too.

Now's the time to start thinking rich; learning how to get rich; taking actions to become rich and stay rich; and finding ways to share riches for a more meaningful life. Begin with the correct mindset and money beliefs, cultivate successful habits, and apply the timeless rules of wealth that this book teaches.

If you live by the principles of wealth, you'll be on the way to financial success—slowly but surely.

Ready to begin your journey to greater prosperity and happiness? Read on and go for it!

PART ONE

THINK RICH

I have about concluded that wealth is a state of mind, and that anyone can acquire a wealthy state of mind by thinking rich thoughts.
—Edward Young

The Global Wealth Report published by the Credit Suisse Research Institute found that there are 52 million millionaires (end 2019) worldwide. While this figure may appear as if there are many rich people around, but with 7.8 billion people living on this planet today, millionaires only represent about 0.6% of the world population. Even in advanced economies in which opportunities abound, there are so few wealthy people. Why aren't there more rich people in the world? What's more, most people can't achieve financial independence and might even need to delay their retirement!

People talk a lot about wealth. But they don't seem to be able to achieve it for some elusive reasons. I strongly believe that the most important reason why people don't become rich has got something to do with their mind—it has never occurred to them that it's possible for them to be wealthy in the first place. And because they don't believe they could be wealthy, they never choose to take any progressive steps to become rich. That being the case, how can people ever become wealthy?

How many times have you heard parents telling their children to study hard, get a good degree, and work hard at your job to ensure a successful life? Your parents probably had told you the same thing too when you were a child. That's outdated advice because it doesn't always work in today's economy. The truth is, most people have been conditioned to believe that studying hard and working long hours are good indicators of a successful future. They are being told that saving as much money as possible is the key to riches. They couldn't be more wrong!

We have been conditioned to think wrongly about how to be wealthy and successful. Don't get me wrong. I'm not against anyone studying hard to get a good degree. Neither am I implying that working hard isn't good. These are all important. At the very least, a good degree could improve the chances of getting a higher-paid job. And working hard is essential in achieving success in life. But just having a good education and working hard won't make you rich. Otherwise, the percentage of millionaires around the world would be much higher than the figure that was reported. You need to start with a correct mindset and manage your finances wisely if you are to become wealthy.

Many people have dysfunctional beliefs and thoughts about money. They have been taught to believe that money is scarce—hard to earn, harder to make, and hardest to keep. We must shift our money mindset from scarcity to abundance. Wealth creation is 80% mental and 20% actions. Mastering money and wealth creation hinge more on mindset than anything else. That is why it is important to start with a correct money mindset before you even start building your wealth.

1

The Meaning of Wealth

The beginning of wisdom is the definition of terms.
—Socrates

What Is Wealth to You?

Most people have hazy ideas of what wealth is. When I asked people around me what wealth is to them, many vaguely define it as "earning a lot of money". If you happen to define wealth this way too, you are not totally incorrect though. But how much is "a lot of money" to you?

To some people, earning $5,000 a month is a lot of money; more than enough to sustain their frugal lives. To others, even a $20,000 per month salary is considered little if the amount isn't sufficient to finance their really posh lifestyles.

For one to be wealthy, it doesn't necessary means that the person must be a millionaire. Wealth shouldn't be just about dollars and cents. It should also include the ability to experience life and live it to the fullest. When it comes to wealth, money sometimes plays a smaller role than what most people believe. Take my late mother-in-law as an example. She valued family and friends above everything else. Whenever she was spending time with her family or good friends, she would have felt as though she was the richest person on earth. Clearly, wealth to her meant being surrounded by people she cherished. And she wouldn't have exchanged it with anything that would take away her quality time with loved ones.

People can feel wealthy when they have a happy family. Others may consider themselves wealthy because they manage to escape the rat race, and have enough income to live the life they have always wanted. Hence, wealth means different things to different people. It's personal and has to be clearly defined by you, not by others, or how the various media portray wealthy people to be. For me, being wealthy means having the freedom to do what I enjoy; having the time to spend with whom I like; and being able to do all these without worrying about whether I have enough money to cover all my expenses.

How do you define wealth? Clearly define what wealth is to you before you start pursuing it. Your personal definition of wealth is exactly what this book, *The Principles of Wealth*, will mean to you. From here onwards, the word "wealth" as used in this book will be according to how you interpret wealth. Your wealth definition will act as a compass to give you the directions to reach your financial goals. It will also help you determine your saving goals, spending budget, and the various investment strategies that suit your needs.

The true meaning of wealth moves beyond your net worth. It's about meaning, purpose, and living life on your terms. Wealth, over and above money, could also include time, relationship, experience and other things that matters to the person. What most people truly want is not only riches, but happiness and health as well.

Income Is Not Wealth

Many people confuse income with wealth. Income is not the same as wealth. In broad terms, income is what you earn, while wealth is how much you keep and accumulate. To elaborate further in economic terms, wealth is the net worth of an individual—the value of all his assets minus all his liabilities. Income, on the other hand, is the total amount of money an individual receives including salary, wages, interests, dividends, rents, and any other earnings.

Unfortunately, while most of us are taught how to earn income getting jobs, we are never taught how to manage our money; how to invest to grow our money; and how to accumulate and keep wealth. The lack of financial intelligence causes most people to be poor stewards of their finances, and because of this, the majority of people couldn't get wealthy in their lifetime. Whether a person is rich or not doesn't depend on how huge the person's salary is. A lot depends on how the money is being used and the way it is invested. When income increases, people have a tendency to increase their spending as well. This could spiral into dangerous overspending habits arising from the upgrading of their lifestyle.

What matters most isn't how much money people make; it is how much money they can keep. People who earn huge salaries doesn't mean they're wealthy, especially if they spend more just to maintain their high standards of living. On the contrary, people who earn less could be living frugally, thus allowing them to save more money to be used for creating wealth through investments. Wealth is created by spending money to buy assets or things that can generate additional income. Smart investors get money working hard for them. Anyone who doesn't save to invest won't be able to create substantial wealth in the long run, even if he or she earns high income.

Let me cite two examples to illustrate the difference between income and wealth...

The Poor High-Income Earner

Jeremy is a regional sales director of a multinational corporation. He earns an income of around $300,000 a year. I must say that's quite an impressive salary even by today's standard. But Jeremy isn't wealthy. Surprise? Or even shock? Yes, it's true. Jeremy isn't rich. Yet to be if hope is factored in. Read on and you'll know why.

With his high income, Jeremy and his family lives the high life. They reside in a big landed house in an upper-class district. His house is estimated to be worth about $5 million. Jeremy has two children, a son and a daughter, both in their early teens. His children are studying in an expensive international school.

Outside school, his son takes violin lessons while his daughter attends ballet classes. A tennis coach is also hired to teach Jeremy's children play better tennis, twice on weeknights and once during the weekends.

Jeremy enjoys playing golf. He goes to various golf courses with his friends for golfing sessions on most weekends. Since he has a passion for the game, Jeremy also purchased two prestigious golf and country club memberships as well.

What about the cars his family own? Well, Jeremy drives a Mercedes-Benz S400 while his wife drives a BMW X5. Both cars are purchased brand new.

Jeremy's family takes exotic vacations two to three times every year. His wife loves travelling to Milan for her shopping spree. And she does that once every year.

A very admirable life indeed!

Judging by Jeremy's lifestyle, together with the "assets" that the family own, people would definitely think that they are very wealthy. Without a doubt, their outward appearances certainly look impressive.

However, Jeremy's high income also comes with an equally high family spending—a huge mortgage and auto loans for the two luxury cars; children's expenses for education, violin lessons, ballet classes and tennis coaching sessions; golf and country club memberships; exotic vacations; expensive meals; together with other miscellaneous expenses. Now, these expenses can really add up to an astronomical amount! What's more, Jeremy's monthly spending sometimes exceeds the income that he earns. So, he uses credit to finance his spending. With such excessive expenditure, it isn't surprising that he lives paycheck to paycheck, despite his respectable salary. If Jeremy loses his job, with no more paychecks coming, he will be broke in no time.

The Wealthy Average Income Earner

George works as an assistant manager in a fast-moving consumer goods company. His salary isn't very high by today's standard—about $55,000 per annum. But he is wealthy. George and his family live a simple, frugal life. George drives a small and modest car, saves about 20% of his income, and pays credit card bills in full every month. He invests his savings diligently by buying bonds, dividend-paying stocks, and real estate investment trusts (REITs). He also bought another house some years ago, which has been leased for rental income.

After investing for more than 20 years, George managed to build up an investment portfolio worth approximately $1.2 million. He and his wife have recently paid off the mortgage of their small 3-bedroom condominium they are residing in. They are not planning to upgrade to a bigger house. George and his family may not be living a lavish life. They may not appear rich from the outside, but they are certainly rich on the inside!

Not only are George and his family living comfortably, they are free from consumer debt too. In fact, both George and his wife never have to worry about money anymore since the income generated from their investments can finance their current frugal lives.

George and his wife are still having full-time jobs. But they remain employed because they choose to, not because they need to. Both of them have the option to retire anytime they wish. In other words, they are not only rich, but have also achieved financial freedom.

Wealth Creation Needs Discipline, Not High Income

I hope the above examples of Jeremy and George would help clarify the differences between income and wealth. Building wealth doesn't require a large income, but it certainly requires discipline as well as commitment to manage finances wisely. Wealth generates income for the shrewd investors, making them richer by the day. A high salary can only help an individual appear wealthy if money is spent on material things recklessly instead of being invested. Careless high spenders will only make someone else rich, while they stay cash-strapped.

Earning a huge salary doesn't guarantee financial success unless the high-income earner uses part of the income to invest in assets that generate additional income. Income creates wealth only if it is well-managed and invested wisely.

Why Do You Want to Be Rich?

Have you ever asked yourself why do you want to be rich? You're not alone if you haven't done so. Most people never ask themselves this question either. But I think it's important that you determine the reasons for wanting to be rich. That way, you'll get to know your purpose in life and what to do with your wealth. I have posed this question to people from all walks of life. The same question drew different answers that were as diverse as the people being asked. Let's check out their responses...

I once asked Jack, my car mechanic, what he would do if he's rich. Showing some excitement, he replied, "I shall quit my job immediately! I'll then buy a big house, a Ferrari, and travel round the world. Yeah, I'll do nothing and just enjoy life!" I guess he might have been dreaming about becoming rich for some years already. Otherwise, he wouldn't have responded with such spontaneity and enthusiasm. But I doubt the lifestyle that he hopes for is sustainable; and that his happiness would last long. I have a friend, a former chief operation officer of a multinational corporation, who quitted his job and spent much of his life traveling. About three years on, he became bored and started to find no meaning in the way he was living his life. Eventually, he came out of retirement and ventured into a new business with his friends.

A product manager of a food manufacturing company, when asked what he will do with riches, unreservedly answered me, "If I ever become rich one day, I shall buy this company and fire my boss!" From his simple answer, I can deduce that he hates his boss very much. There's a good chance that the manager has been treated so badly while working for his boss, so much so that he wants to own the company just to get rid of his boss. There may well be many others wanting to start up their own businesses for the very same reason as this manager—to be the boss so he can do whatever he likes. However, no one doing business can actually be his own boss. Why? Any business would need customers to buy their products to flourish, and because of this fact, any customer would naturally become the boss of the business owner!

Another lady, who is working as a receptionist in a small company, replied: "I'm very satisfied with my job. It's easy work and I knock off at exactly 5:00 p.m. every day. And I haven't got much work stress. Nah, I'm not interested mixing with those snobbish, greedy and conceited high-life people in their tuxedos. I've got no interest in what they do. It's just not for me and I'm happy where I am." Just like this receptionist, people with such attitude are unlikely to make changes to go to another level of their life. They prefer the status quo and would resist anything that could threaten their relaxed way of life.

Yet another friend of mine, a stay-at-home mom, when asked what she would do if she becomes wealthy, said: "Many friends I know don't have much money. They aren't enjoying the best things in life. If I'm rich, I would love to bless them, bring them to taste some great cuisine at fine restaurants. And for some of them, they have been so stressed and seriously overworked, I wish to pay for their holiday trips with their family so they could relax a bit and rejuvenate. I can't bring money with me after I pass on, right? So, I might as well try to bless as many people as I could." Her response deeply touched my heart. She is truly a warm-hearted lady blessed with a noble heart. She understood that happiness comes from giving, not buying and having!

From the various responses, we could see people desire riches for different reasons, and for different motives. To be sure, there will also be people rejecting wealth for personal reasons. But those are exceptions rather than the norm.

You have to figure out why you wish to become wealthy. Is it to satisfy your selfish desires? Or are you going to make a difference in society? Are you pursuing riches at the expense of your family? Or will you set aside time to date your spouse and spend more quality time with your family?

State the reasons for wanting to be wealthy in order to uncover your true motives. Your purpose for this wealth will be your driver and your motivation to be rich. With a better and clearer understanding of your purpose and motives, you can be mindful to balance time as well as to take corrective actions, if necessary, in your pursuit of wealth.

Always remember that money isn't the end goal. You are making money because of what you'll do with it. Money is simply a tool. And nothing more!

2

Wrong Money Beliefs

All riches have their origin in mind. Wealth is in ideas, not money.
—Robert Collier

How many times have you heard people saying, "Money does not grow on tree?" Try asking the apple growers and see if they agree with you. I'm pretty sure business owners in the pulp and paper industry wouldn't agree to that saying too. All of us grow up with money beliefs, some of which are myths that need to be addressed if we want any breakthrough in our finances. We get a lot of those beliefs from the way our parents brought us up.

The biggest stumbling block to wealth and its creation is negative money beliefs. If we think we can't achieve wealth, we won't. Therefore, we must examine our beliefs to determine whether any changes to our thoughts about money are required. We need to unlearn some of the wrong beliefs that may still be ingrained in us. Below are some common wrong beliefs and attitudes toward money and wealth that many people have:

- Wealth corrupts
- It is better to be poor and happy than to be rich and sad
- Rich people are greedy, selfish and dishonest
- Getting rich is largely about luck
- You are not righteous if you are wealthy

- You must have lots of money to make money
- Money does not buy happiness
- You must be born rich to be wealthy
- Rich people are unhappy people
- The more you have, the more you will want
- Rich people do not enjoy happy relationships
- Money is the root of all evil

How many of the above statements are in your belief system? Are there any money myths you need to dispel?

Does Money Buy Happiness?

One of the most common myths we often hear is that money does not buy happiness. This statement is only partially true. While it's true to some extent that money doesn't buy you happiness, not having money isn't paradise for you either. Let's be honest. Would you be happy if you don't have enough money to put food on the table each day? Would you be happy if you can't afford to bring your loved ones for a vacation? Would you be happy if you are constantly worrying about money, and having sleepless nights because of it? I'm sure you won't be. Having more money certainly makes it easier for you to live a more complete and happier life.

Money might not buy you happiness directly. But then, don't you agree that it's more comfortable to cry in a Rolls-Royce than on a bicycle? We need to recognize that even though money may not buy happiness in some instances, neither can poverty. Any normal and sane person would want money to serve him well. There is really nothing wrong in using money to live a more comfortable life.

Do You Need Lots of Money to Start With?

Another popular belief is that it takes a lot of money to make money. This belief simply doesn't hold water. Take the low cost of this book as an example. Put in some effort to read and learn; sprinkle a little creativity; add some hard work and self-discipline; and wealth will be yours.

Consider this rags-to-riches story of Jack Ma—the Chinese billionaire who founded Alibaba (China's answer to Amazon). Ma was born in a very poor family in Hangzhou, located in the southeastern part of China. He failed his university-entrance examination twice. Ma then went on to apply for 30 different jobs and got rejected, including one at Kentucky Fried Chicken where 24 people applied for the job and 23 got hired (with him being the only one rejected), before finding success with his third internet company, Alibaba Group. Ma is one of the wealthiest men in the world today. According to *Forbes*, he has a net worth of $58.2 billion as of January 2019.

If there is any truth in that we need lots of money to make more money, I would need to rewrite my own history. Here's my story in a nutshell—born in a lower-middle class family, poor along the way, retired a millionaire. I have very little money to begin with. It is my savings which I used for investing that makes me rich when my investments bear fruits over time.

American minister and author, Norman Vincent Peale, said it aptly, "Empty pockets never held anyone back. Only empty heads and empty hearts can do that."

Is Money Evil?

Money is one of those taboo subjects hardly discussed among family and friends. Even married couples often shun the topic on money because it's deemed to be sensitive. I often hear people say "money destroys marriages" and "money destroys lives." But is money really evil?

The common saying "money is the root of all evil" is often misquoted and taken out of context. Here's the verse from the Bible taken from 1 Timothy 6:10 (King James Version): "For the love of money is the root of all evil: which while some coveted after, they have erred from the faith, and pierced themselves through with many sorrows." Notice what is actually written in the verse? It's the *love* of money and certainly not money itself that is the root of all evil. More often than not, it's financial struggles that destroys marriages and lives. In other words, the *lack* of money is frequently the root of all evil.

T. Harv Eker, author and businessman known for his theories on wealth and motivation, once said, "Money will only make you more of what you already are. If you're mean, money will afford you the opportunity to be meaner. If you're kind, money will afford you the opportunity to be kinder." Money is just a medium of exchange and a means to an end. It's neither good or evil. Money has no power in itself. Can your money in the bank do evil things when left alone? Of course not! It can only earn you interest, and helps you take on other types of investments when you have sufficient of it in the future.

Money in itself is completely amoral. Take the knife as an example. Is the knife good or evil? If you use the knife to cut fruits for your family to eat, then the knife becomes a tool for good. However, if you take the knife out and use it to kill someone, it would then become an instrument of evil! Again, the knife is amoral, neither good nor evil, depending on how we use it.

The same applies for money. If you use $5,000 to buy cocaine, the money is used for evil. But when you spend the $5,000 for a family vacation, then the money is used for good by facilitating family bonding.

Therefore, it's not the money but the person behind the money that determines its characteristics. If you are a righteous person, you'll put the money to good use. If you are wicked, you'll probably use the money for evil purposes. Money is only evil if you are evil!

Make Money Your Friend

We must acknowledge the fact that the world can't function without money. Despising money doesn't do much for our society. Likewise, remaining poor will not do us or the people around us good. Everybody needs money to pay mortgages, pay utility bills, pay medical bills, pay for food, pay for education, and the list goes on. Money, therefore, is needed by everybody and plays a very significant role in our lives. We should treat money as our friend and not our enemy. We just need to master over money and put it to good use.

Consider some of the good things money can offer:

- Provides you with the ability to do charitable deeds
- Enables you to better serve and impact people around you
- Frees up your time so you can focus on what truly matters to you
- Allows you to work because you *want* to and not because you *need* to
- Ends your sleepless nights without having to worry about your finances
- Provides a better and more comfortable life for you and your loved ones
- Gives you a peace of mind knowing you are able to cover any unexpected emergencies

It is actually much easier to be poor than it is to be rich. But do you seriously want to take the path of least resistance? If you choose the easier path, it won't lead you to anything that you are genuinely seeking. Sure, people who are poor may still be able to donate money for a good cause, despite a smaller amount. However, isn't it much better for people to be wealthy so they could give even more to charity?

Don't make money your enemy. Master over money instead. You just need to ensure that money doesn't control you and your life. And it definitely makes good sense to have money as your ally so it can help you achieve your desired goals in life.

Build Wealth Being Good

There are many examples of wealthy people living on their ill-gotten gains. The *Forbes* list of world's billionaires is brimming over with oligarchs, hustlers, thugs, and miscreants. Don't be one of them. Never make money by breaking laws, cheating, ripping people off, being dishonest, compromising principles, or by any other illegal means. I'm sure you want to sleep well at night without having to fret over when the police would come knocking at your door to arrest you. You want to become wealthy knowing that your riches are gained in a legitimate, fair and honest way, won't you? I believe you also wish to have healthy relationships with people who can believe and trust you with any business dealings.

Wealth creation, and the way money is used, have the potential to spread and increase wealth in general. It can be like the rising tide in the sea that lifts all boats. Wealth isn't scarce. And it surely isn't a limited resource. When the creation of wealth is done correctly, it need not necessarily be a situation where a person's gain is another person's loss.

Let's remove the stigma of being wealthy once and for all. Wealth isn't good or bad—it's the person that makes it one or the other. What many people lack is a clear understanding of why they want wealth for themselves, and how they want to use the riches gained. If you love people and use money, you've got it right.

On the contrary, if you love money and use people, you've got everything wrong! Therefore, it's how you deal with people and what you use the money for that matters most.

Get Rid of All Wrong Money Beliefs

If you buy into any of the wrong money beliefs and attitudes, you could be held back from making some serious money. Try to remember the people who are responsible for programming those wrong money beliefs in your mind. If you have identified those people, ask yourself if they're richer or more successful than you. It makes sense that if you want a solution to a problem, seek advice and listen to people who are more than qualified to provide you with solutions. Would you ask the doctor to fix your car? I bet you won't. Similarly, I don't believe you would go to the car mechanic to get medical advice. However, you'll be surprise to find out that many people actually seek guidance from people who are poor or have very little money.

Studies have shown that people with negative attitudes about wealth are generally people who don't have much money. Wealthy people are unlikely to have any of the money myths already highlighted earlier. More often than not, the wealthy would have gotten rid of those wrong beliefs if they had. Should you still have wrong beliefs and attitudes towards money and wealth, it will do you good to purge them to give yourself a better chance of becoming wealthy. Rich thoughts are necessary for anyone who wants to be financially successful.

So, let me ask you again, "Do you want to be wealthy?" It is perfectly alright to admit that you want to. If you want to do good, being wealthy is one of the ways to make doing good possible, and easier, than if you are poor.

It is also fine if you don't have the desire to pursue material affluence. But then again, do yourself and others a favor—please don't criticize, discourage or worst still, condemn others who wish to pursue riches to accomplish good. The world needs more people who are willing to use their riches to further good causes. It also needs more people to develop a healthier attitude toward wealth.

3

Why Are Most People Not Rich?

Rich people believe "You can have your cake and eat it too."
Middle-class people believe "Cake is too rich, so I'll only have a little piece."
Poor people don't believe they deserve cake, so they order a doughnut,
focus on the hole, and wonder why they have "nothing".
—T. Harv Eker

Is a fat paycheck the only way for a person to become rich? Certainly not! It's never about how much a person is capable of earning. Rather, it's how much money a person can keep. Sure, there will be people who received a windfall by winning the lottery. Maybe some lucky ones will get large inheritances from unknown relatives and suddenly become rich.

There are also people who become rich and famous by marrying the rich and famous. Still, some others could get rich by sheer luck. Somehow, the majority of us don't happen to be one of these lucky ones!

I often wonder. In countries where opportunities abound, why is it that most people of those nations aren't rich? And why is it that the majority of people living in advanced economies won't be retiring financially free?

It's a sad fact that many people may never become wealthy in their lifetime, even though they are presented with opportunities to make money or accumulate wealth. Many people missed or choose to ignore the many wonderful opportunities in their lifetime, just because those opportunities are clothed in hard work. Wealth isn't discriminatory for the selected few. It is everywhere waiting for people to acquire. But it seems that those people who acquire wealth are the ones who wake up early, work hard and put in the efforts. After spending many years researching and observing the lives of both the rich and the poor, I find that most people aren't wealthy not because of a lack of opportunity, but rather a result of their own doings.

Let's explore some common reasons why the majority of people don't get rich...

Procrastination

A major reason why people don't get rich is because they tend to procrastinate. Most people may have thoughts of becoming rich. But when the time calls for necessary actions, they come up with all kinds of lame excuses for not being able to manage their finances well.

For the procrastinators, there will always be a good enough reason to delay doing what is important for achieving financial success. It's always the wrong day, wrong month, or the wrong season. They will say, "Better to wait until the economy improves before taking action. Maybe next year would be a better time." Seemingly good reasons are always readily available to those wanting to procrastinate. As a result, most people keep putting off the things they need to do, day by day, month by month, year by year, until it is too late.

Procrastination will always push your financial plans into the indefinite future. For the sake of your financial security, never put off until tomorrow what you can do today. Always keep in mind that your income can only grow to the extent that you do. So, don't procrastinate any longer, and follow what the Nike slogan says—Just Do It!

Too Lazy to Be Rich

Many people dream of being rich and famous, but never take any further action beyond that. A dream would remain a dream if no work is ever done to realize it.

It's a fact that most people are just too lazy to get rich. The thought of all the hard work that is involved turns them off. They rather spend time watching TV, playing computers games, watching YouTube videos, or just lazing around doing nothing. They are not prepared to work hard, make sacrifices, learn, research, and do whatever it takes to create wealth. Lazy people want all the money, but without all the hard work that comes along. Gamblers or those who buy lottery tickets with the hope of getting rich overnight do so for the very same reason—they want to be wealthy without doing any work.

If you examine some of the wealthiest people in this world like Bill Gates, Warren Buffett, and Richard Branson, you'll find that they are all very hardworking and committed people. Whatever these rich tycoons are doing, they do much more than anyone else. They work hard, smart, and efficiently. They don't waste any time doing unproductive things. It really seems like they're able to do more in a day than most people can do in a month!

These ultra-successful individuals are living examples to show us that if we want to be rich, commitment, discipline and hard work are unavoidable. Anyone can be wealthy—that person basically needs to work for it more than the next person does.

Many people simply don't take any action to do what's necessary to make them rich. Even if they read books, listen to audio books, attend seminars, participate in workshops, hire financial coaches, or even associate with financially people, nothing will change until they decide to take actions to improve their current financial situation. Knowledge without action is pointless and no real change can ever occur. There is no point hoping, praying, or merely wishing to get rich one day if you don't act. You must make a definite commitment, put in the effort, and work tirelessly to achieve your wealth goals.

WHY ARE MOST PEOPLE NOT RICH?

Underachievement or failure are often the end results when people don't decide to take solid actions to be successful. If you keep doing the same thing over and over again, don't expect different results. Do note that the only place where you can find success before work is in the dictionary—where the word "success" would appear before the word "work." Other than that, there is really no such thing as effortless success. Success surely demands work!

Being Wealthy Is Only a Wish

How many people actually make it a priority in life to become wealthy? During my younger days as a student, I often heard my fellow schoolmates talking about making it big in life, and becoming rich by 30. But talk is just talk, and it remains as that if no action is taken to work towards achieving the success they spoke about.

People who just talk without any action won't accomplish anything of value in life. The underachievers spend most of their time talking, or just wishing, without spending much time doing the things that help achieve the desired results. On the contrary, the wealthy will never waste time talking, they spend most of their time working hard to meet their goals.

If you want to be wealthy, you must take immediate steps to manage and control your finances actively—like cutting down unnecessary expenses, building up your savings, reducing debts (especially the bad ones), and investing to accumulate assets. Have you already started doing these things?

How badly do you want wealth? Is it bad enough to forgo buying those fanciful gadgets; eating less frequently at fine dining restaurants; cutting down on fine wines; or not buying an Audi but settling instead for an entry-level Toyota?

Cutting excessive spending would allow you to save money. The earlier you save, the earlier you can have cash to invest and take advantage of the power of compound interest. And the earlier you gain excess cash from investment profits, the earlier you can start accumulating more assets to make you richer.

Who, Me? Don't Think So!

Another reason why most people don't become wealthy is that they never think it's possible for them to become rich. Let's dig deeper and try to find out why they believe so.

The average person:

- has grown up in an average household;
- has never known anyone wealthy;
- has no role models who are wealthy;
- socializes with people who are not wealthy;
- works with people who are not wealthy;
- has a social circle consisting of people who are not wealthy.

Most people have little exposure to wealthy people to adopt any wealth values. With the absence of wealth guidance for most people—from birth through to formative years, and then continued till mature adults—they might come to believe that it is a far-fetched dream for them to be rich one day.

It's worth noting that children with wealthy parents are more likely to become rich when they grow up to be adults compared with those who grew up in poor families. However, let me qualify that this is just a general trend, and exceptions surely exist. I'm sure you have come across many true stories of people who went from rags to riches despite being born into poor families.

When you are mostly surrounded by people who aren't that successful, it becomes easy for you to pick up poor habits, together with all the wrong ideas concerning wealth. That is why most people need to unlearn many money myths they have grown up with, or picked up along the way from those with poor money habits. It definitely helps to surround yourself with successful people so that you can possibly rub off some rich habits and financial knowledge from them. Whenever possible, stay away from pessimistic people; especially the negatively "still" ones—those who are still complaining, still jealous, still hating, still lazy, still broke, and still nowhere. Flee from these negative people!

WHY ARE MOST PEOPLE NOT RICH?

All of us hold the keys to our own destinies. We will only remain in the same state if we allow it. Poor people are never condemned to be poor forever. It's possible for anyone to become wealthy with the right mindset, skills and appropriate actions.

Overspend Using Credit

The world generally classifies people into two categories—the *haves* and the *have-nots*. The haves are people with lots of money while the have-nots consist of those with very little. However, I would like to highlight a third category—the "have not paid for what they have"—that is frequently overlooked. After analyzing the statistics on credit card spending and payment patterns, I'm convinced that many people should appropriately be classified in this third category.

Media promoting easy credit to live an expensive lifestyle causes many to develop ill-disciplined spending habits. With so many people everywhere spending more than they can afford, would it even come as a surprise that many people would need to extend retirement due to insufficient savings? What's more, these people are likely to be one paycheck away from bankruptcy!

For many years, credit cards that are in circulation have been increasing steadily. Same goes for the average household credit card debt. Credit card rollover balance (the outstanding amount subjected to interest charges) also spiraled upwards. Such trends reflect the popularity of easy credit, with consumers flashing plastic without paying the bills fully month after month. If these people continue to spend everything they earn, or worst, use credit to spend $2.00 for every $1.00 they make, how can they ever be rich? Are they hoping to keep their jobs forever? Or are they planning never to retire? Ask them!

Never treat the use of credit card for spending spree as a lifestyle. It isn't chic. Not when you're are trying to get out of debt and build wealth.

Having a mountain of debt and living paycheck to paycheck will prevent anyone from getting rich. You must exercise discipline not to spend more than you earn. Otherwise, riches will evade you and you'll never end up wealthy in your lifetime.

4

It's All in the Mind

The mind is the limit. As long as the mind can envision the fact that you can do something, you can do it, as long as you really believe 100 percent.
—Arnold Schwarzenegger

After spending many years examining the traits of wealthy people—most of them not born into rich families—I can come to a conclusion that people become wealthy because they possess a rich mindset. There are reasons why people become wealthy. Nothing happens by chance and certainly, people don't become rich because they're just lucky. I'm not talking about those who gained riches by winning the lottery, that's another topic to be discussed later. Rather, I'm referring to people who deliberately plan to become wealthy and take actions to ensure they reach their goals.

Whether someone would move on to be financially successful, or be constantly broke, is determined by the person's mindset. An individual's mindset is an important trait in determining one's destiny.

Develop a Rich Mindset

The difference between the rich and the poor is the way in which they think. If you think rich, you can become rich when your mind is set out to achieve your wealth goals. On the other hand, if you have poor thoughts, your limiting beliefs would work against you in your quest for wealth.

The table below compares the differences between the mindset of the rich and that of the poor:

RICH MINDSET	POOR MINDSET
Always makes a plan	Always makes an excuse
Sees possibilities	Sees problems
Sees an answer for every problem	Sees a problem for every answer
Makes commitments	Makes promises
Makes things happen	Let things happen
Makes mistakes but says "I was wrong!"	Makes mistakes but says "It wasn't my fault!"
Says "I must do something!"	Says "Something must be done!"
Says "It may be difficult but it's possible!"	Says "It may be possible but it's too difficult!"
Says "How to minimize the risks?"	Says "There're too much risks involved!"
Says "How can I afford it?"	Says "I can't afford it!"
Says "How can I get it done?"	Says "I can't do it!"

Notice the difference between how the poor and the rich think on the various issues? The rich are both committed and passionate in whatever they set out to do. Most importantly, rich and successful people believe in themselves and they don't find excuses to deter them from pursuing their goals. You must be prepared to change your thinking, be fully committed, and put in the necessary efforts to achieve success.

Your Current Mindset Determines Your Future Destiny

Your mindset (set of beliefs that you hold dear) determines your perspective (how you see things). Wealthy people see things differently from what others normally see. They see opportunities in all areas of their lives when others can only see problems. A millionaire stumbling upon a pile of scrap metals could see the making of a wonderful sculpture for the collector's market.

To the rich, problems that they encounter could present opportunities for greater prosperity. They are not limited by the circumstances surrounding them.

The following story best illustrates this point...

A shoe factory owner sent his two sons, Peter and Paul, to a faraway land to explore the market potential for shoes. After a few weeks, both sons returned and reported their observations to their father. Peter said, "Father, it's impossible to market our shoes in that land because those people walk bare-footed. They don't wear shoes, so how could they like shoes? Nobody is going to buy our shoes!" Paul, on the other hand, got very excited and reported, "Dad, it's a gold mine out there! Since none of them are wearing shoes now, everybody can be our potential customers. The market is huge so let's start convincing those people to buy our shoes!"

The optimism displayed by Paul in the story provides valuable lessons for us. It's never the situation that is at fault. It's always the way we choose to view it.

Change Your Perspective to Change Your Life

Do you see the glass half full or half empty? How you see the world and how you interpret different situations will determine your actions, reactions and decisions. Really, you do have control over your mind to some extent. If some areas of your life are not working well for you, changing your perspective on the situations could make a big difference.

We need to be more optimistic, and learn to see things from a different perspective. See opportunities during times of crisis. See the positives in the negatives. See the future in the present. Assess further to see if there is a way to take advantage of a situation instead of being hampered by it. A research conducted by Suzanne Segerstrom, a Professor of Psychology at the University of Kentucky, found that optimists are happier, healthier and richer.

If you want to get rich, you must first develop the mindset of the rich. It's very important because the kind of mindset you have will eventually determine your future course and destiny. A simple shift in your mindset can point you in the right direction to becoming as wealthy as you want to be.

Now, please answer the following questions as honestly as you possibly can:

- Do you want to earn more income or pursue your passion doing work you love?
- Do you want to buy your dream house or make a big donation to a charity?
- Do you want a successful career or a close relationship with your family?
- Do you want to save more money or bring your family to a long vacation?
- Do you want to be rich or do you want to be healthy?

What are your answers to the questions?

My answers would be "both" to all the questions, and I hope your answers are the same too. You really don't have to choose one or the other, especially when given a choice between two equally attractive options. Why not have the cake and eat it too? It's possible. Try to achieve both instead.

An important point to take note though. When I suggest that you choose both given options, I'm certainly not saying that you should operate this way in every situation. For instance, assuming you are shopping for a watch and are deciding between a Rolex or an Omega, should you just buy both watches? I think you shouldn't. Not unless you're a millionaire. If you desire a new watch but don't have the cash to pay fully, or perhaps you still have outstanding consumer debts yet to pay, I suggest you buy none of those luxurious watches. Go and buy yourself a Seiko instead.

Wealthy people know that with an open mind and a willingness to be unconventional, they can have both options. While the rich live in a world of abundance, the poor live in a world of scarcity and focus on limitations instead.

When you develop the powerful habit of "thinking both," you will suddenly see opportunities that you were once blind to. Hence, if you wish to achieve both options rather than limiting yourself to just one, all you need is the right mindset to get there.

The right frame of mind can get you motivated, focused, committed, and disciplined to realize your goals. Ultimately, success will be yours to enjoy!

Is It More Important to Be Rich or Happy?

I once asked several of my friends whether being rich or being happy is more important to them. Guess what? All of them indicated that being happy is more important than being rich. What about you? Did you just choose happiness as well?

Paused for a moment to think a bit deeper before you readily agree with their answers. Then, ask yourself the following questions:

- Would you be happy if you are constantly starving without cash to buy more food?
- Would you be happy if you can't afford medical treatment when illness befalls you?
- Would you be happy if you can't clothe yourself adequately?
- Would you be happy if you can't afford a much-needed family holiday?
- Would you be happy if you don't have extra money to buy gifts for your loved ones on special occasions?
- Would you be happy if you lose the roof over your head and need to sleep on the pavement every night?

I certainly won't be happy in any of the above scenarios. I'm sure you'll feel the same too. Sure, it is easier for people to state their preference for happiness over wealth, especially if they are well-to-do individuals living in comfortable conditions. However, would it be as easy for the poor to claim the same? I doubt so. Hence, whether you choose riches or happiness will depend on your current living standards—whether you are living comfortably or living in poor conditions.

First, let's define who the "poor" are. The poor have little or no money, goods or other means of support. When people are poor, they are more concern about meeting their basic needs such as food and shelter. Their priorities are getting the stomach filled and maintaining a roof over the head. What matters most is financial security because without money, the poor can't even survive! As the late Zig Ziglar, a great American author and motivational speaker, once said, "Money is not everything but it ranks right up there with oxygen." Therefore, to the poor, being rich is much more important than being happy.

For those with basic needs already met, most people would start to pursue their "wants" and other luxuries. It is beyond "needs" that they are after. They are likely to be chasing after more money just to keep up with the Joneses. In doing so, these people work harder, sleep lesser, and barely spend quality time with their families. They experience intense pressures and feel stressed out. How can these people be happy even after they become more affluent? Therefore, to most well-off people, being happy is much more important than being rich.

It would be more difficult for people to be happy unless they start living instead of merely existing. Happiness will only come about when the basic needs of people are met. So, is it more important to be rich or to be happy? I would say both are equally important. Sure, I do agree that money can't buy happiness, but the lack of money would cause much unhappiness as well.

There will always be people who are rich and unhappy. Similarly, there will also be people who are poor and happy. But bear in mind that there will certainly be much more people in this world who are poor and unhappy! Rather than limiting your options, why not aim to be both rich and happy? Yes, it is definitely much better to be rich and happy. Don't you agree?

However, if you are only looking to riches to make you happy, I can guarantee you will be sorely disappointed. Money alone doesn't make you happy. It can only buy away a lot of unhappiness. There are other factors—such as family, friends, spirituality, contentment, and success—that play a much more important role in your overall happiness. Happiness is a state of mind. The master switch of happiness is within you. And you alone hold the control to that switch.

5

Attitudes and Habits That Will Make You Rich

If you are going to achieve excellence in big things, you develop the habit in little matters. Excellence is not an exception; it is a prevailing attitude.
—Colin Powell

People are never born successful. They become successful by having great attitudes and forming habits of doing the things unsuccessful people don't like to do. While having excellent attitudes and adopting rich habits may not guarantee that you will become the next millionaire, they can definitely help you live a life full of possibilities. A person's intelligence, skills and talent are certainly significant, but more often than not, these qualities aren't the only factors that separate the wealthy from the rest.

Good attitudes and habits are the foundation of success. Those who are successful differ from unsuccessful ones in their daily habits. Growing your wealth starts with growing yourself, and developing good attitudes and success habits are certainly a great way to start.

Develop a Plan and Execute It

Failing to plan is planning to fail. If you are resolute about being prosperous and successful, you must always have this saying ingrained in your mind. Planning and execution of plans are crucial for accomplishing goals.

A person without a plan trying to achieve his financial goals are akin to him driving a car without a steering wheel, and expecting to reach the desired destination. A plan gives you direction; keeps you focused and motivated; and increase the chances of achieving your goals. Unsuccessful people are likely those without goals, or they have plans but failed to execute any of those plans. On the contrary, people who are successful diligently execute their plans, and keep trying until their goals are met. They are always busy finding new ways to convert their plans into success.

The Things People Talk About

The topics that people enjoy talking about during gatherings or lunch meetings reflect what they are concern about. Generally, the poor like to talk about other people. They gossip about their bosses, colleagues, friends, etc. The middle class like to talk about things. They get excited about cars, holidays, and when the next Apple iPhone is going to be released. Unlike the poor and middle class, who enjoy talking about people and things most of the time, the rich prefer to talk about ideas and inspirations. They don't like wasting time gossiping about other people, and they are certainly not those aiming at being the first to try out the latest gadgets. Wealthy people prefer to discuss and share ideas, probably on how to make money from the poor and the middle class!

So, the next time you sit down with friends to chat over a meal, observe the kind of topics they enjoy talking about, and you will know roughly what type of mindset and attitudes they possess.

The Way People Think

People's way of thinking could determine whether they will find more opportunities or more challenges. Rich people have the habit of thinking positively even during difficult situations.

Positive thinkers find opportunities in the midst of crisis. The poor tend to think in negative ways and hardly take initiatives to do anything new.

People who think positively anticipates happiness, health, wealth and success. Positive thinkers believe in taking actions to overcome any difficulties or obstacles they encounter. Negative thoughts and attitudes can cause unhappy feelings, moods and conducts, which would lead to frustrations, disappointments and failures eventually. Is it any wonder that most people choose to be around positive people and prefer to stay away from the negative ones?

If we want to escape the vicious cycle of poverty, we must develop a positive attitude and change our way of thinking. Think positive and always try to focus on the brighter side of things—even when facing adverse situations.

Don't Fear Change

Change freaks people out so most people shun it as much as they can. Unfortunately, the only thing in this world that remain constant is change. Change applies to many things in your life. Perhaps you are moving to a new house; starting a new job in a different company; migrating to another country; starting or ending a relationship; or lost someone close to you. It's difficult for anyone to avoid change in today's fast-changing world.

Let's get real, change is uncomfortable. Whether it is good or bad, change can cause a certain amount of stress as it involves some adaptations in the way people live their daily lives. Coping with change requires an adjustment on our outlook. Instead of focusing on the negatives that change could bring, we can shift our perspective to see all the positives that come from it.

We experience growth whenever we face, and overcome, challenges in our lives. We can deliberately choose to be grateful for the opportunity to experience life's ups and downs, knowing that every single day, there are millions of unfortunate people out there facing far worse than what we're experiencing.

The rich thrive on change but the poor prefer the tried-and-tested, hesitant of venturing into the unknown. Rather than losing your mind, why not learn to embrace change instead of fearing it?

Swap TV Time for Reading Time

I have many friends who spend many hours, probably 20 to 40 hours per week, watching TV. But most of them don't spend any time reading. When I say watching TV, I'm referring to media consumption in all forms including broadcast television, cable TV, YouTube, Netflix, DVDs, Blu-ray discs, whatever.

I'm not suggesting that you shouldn't watch any TV programs at all, so don't start donating all the television sets in your house. It is true there are many good TV programs worth watching so by all means watch those programs. However, it is absolutely beneficial for you to allocate some time to read on a regular basis too.

Reading will make you smart and creative, just like how food will provide you with nutrients and energy. When you stop reading, you stop having new ideas. Reading is one of the best hobbies that you can take up to become successful.

The wealthy read because they are always striving to improve themselves. Rich people mostly don't have much interest in reading fictions. Instead, they prefer reading nonfiction books which will help them further improve themselves. On the contrary, the poor hardly read; and for those who do read once in a while, they are likely to be reading fictional books. The poor spend more time on the TV instead and they don't consciously seek to develop themselves on a continual basis, unlike the rich.

The rich understand that time is money and will never waste this valuable resource. They choose not to waste time on unnecessary things that don't add value to what they are after. Wealthy people don't spend much time watching TV and even if they do, they will watch mostly intellectual content.

On the other hand, poor people tend to waste more time watching movies, reality shows, or doing other things that won't contribute much to developing themselves for achieving success.

For those who don't read—or who aren't reading regularly—it can be harder to pick up a book than to sit on a comfortable couch to watch TV. Put in some effort to read books and other helpful articles. It pays to enhance your knowledge and wisdom through reading. Consciously make the effort to trade some of your TV time for reading time.

What Separates the Rich from the Poor?

Have you ever wondered what separates the rich from the poor? I have been poor before. But now I am rich. I therefore know both sides very well. Being poor and not yet rich in the past, I yearned to turn my life around and be wealthy. For a very long time, I struggled to believe that I could eventually become wealthy until I realized the differences in thoughts, habits, and attitudes between the rich and the poor. To get a true perspective on how to become wealthy, you must study the mindset and attitudes of rich people, and follow what they do. You become what you study after all.

The wealthy have habits and attitudes that improve themselves and enhance their lives over time. While there may be some extravagant habits of the rich that only wealth can grant access to, there are also simple success habits that the not yet rich can learn to adopt now.

It is hard to be truly successful unless we are aware of our strengths and our weaknesses. We must firstly identify all our daily habits, and then do an honest self-assessment to determine whether these habits are good or bad. Once that is done, we must be willing to make changes if we want to succeed in life.

ATTITUDES AND HABITS THAT WILL MAKE YOU RICH

The following table sums up the attitudes and habits that separate the rich and the poor. Adopting a right attitude, together with rich habits, will help you move in the right direction towards a more successful life.

THE RICH	THE POOR
Are optimistic	Are pessimistic
Are positive thinkers	Are negative thinkers
Take full responsibility; the buck stops here	Deny responsibility; pass the buck
Thrive on change; are willing to change	Prefer the constant; want others to change
Like to analyse	Like to criticise
Listen to others	Talk about others
Have strong self-discipline	Lack self-control
Make money work for them	Work for money
Have both active and passive income	Have only active income
Read a lot	Hardly read

Rich and successful people adopt good attitudes and habits, while eliminating the bad ones that prevent them from achieving their dreams. Remember this: Winning is a habit, so is losing!

6

Complaining Won't Make Things Better

*If you don't like something, change it. If you can't change it,
change your attitude. Don't complain.*
—Maya Angelou

Will complaining makes anything better? Definitely not! Spending today complaining about yesterday won't make tomorrow any better. It is purely a waste of time. Chronic complainers are pessimists who always see a glass half empty. Their constant negativity presents a huge challenge for both themselves as well as the people around them.

Is there any good reason why you should complain frequently? No, not even one. Complaining regularly would only help you remain in a miserable state. Since complaining alone won't help to make your life better, you might as well put your time and energy to better use. Try changing the things you have control over to improve the situation instead.

Making Lemonade Out of Lemons

During the seminars and workshops that I have conducted in the past, I would sometimes put a question to my participants: "What attitude have you brought here today?" Very often,

I received puzzled looks from the audience. I wasn't actually startled though, knowing that most people don't possess a high level of attitude awareness.

I have always been inspired by Nick Vujicic. His positive attitude towards life touches me in a great way and has transformed my perspectives on many things in life.

Vujicic was born without arms or legs. But he has never let his circumstances stop him from living life to the fullest—he lives a life without limits. With only two toes on his left hip, Vujicic is able to pick up things, write, type, shave and even cook. He can play golf, kick football, swim, surf and skydive despite being mainly torso!

However, Vujicic's journey through life wasn't all smooth sailing. As a young boy, he was bullied in school and struggled with depression and loneliness. He was extremely unhappy with his disability and even attempted suicide by trying to drown himself in a bathtub. Thank God his suicide effort failed or we would have lost one of the greatest inspirational speakers in the world.

Undisputedly a symbol of positivity, Vujicic once said, "I have the choice to be angry at God for what I don't have, or be thankful for what I do have." He is now serving God in a mighty way as a messenger of hope. Despite having no limbs, he travels all over the world as a motivational speaker and evangelist, inspiring and touching the lives of millions of people worldwide with his outlook on life. Vujicic even went on to tie the nuptial knot with Kanae Miyahara, and the lovely couple was blessed with not one, but four children!

A positive attitude can change a person's perspective towards his or her situations. Vujicic's display of such an attitude is truly remarkable. He chose to focus on the good that was in his life even when going through his most difficult years in life. He said, "You know, I had all these negative things and a list of things that I couldn't do and I didn't have—so it's powerful when you can embrace what you cannot change, accept it, change the things you can change and know the difference between what you can change and what you can't change. I can't change my disability, but I can change the way I look at it. There are disappointments, there are failures, but I'm not a failure and that's what I encourage myself with." Vujicic's conditions never change, but his perspective on the circumstances certainly has.

Positive attitudes attract positive results while negative attitudes will invite negative results. Winston Churchill said it well: "Attitude is a little thing that makes a big difference." Our attitudes will either make us or break us. No one can control your attitude but you alone. You possess the power to choose whether to have a positive or negative outlook towards life. Importantly, your success is dependent upon the attitude that you bring forth when confronting any issues at hand.

If life throws lemons at you, make lemonade. This popular saying is one that I'll always remind myself of whenever I face obstacles or any other problems. Instead of staring at defeat right at your face, why not face it with courage and make the best out of the situation? Always try to make the best of any negative circumstances. Easier said than done, though, but do we really have better choices or alternatives? We might as well learn how to adopt a more optimistic approach in the face of adversity, and look forward to a more positive outcome that could follow.

Stop Complaining

Few people would remember what life was before, and the people who have always been there even in the most painful situations. Many complain all day, every day, and seem to be addicted to complaining. Studies reveal that the average person complains between 15 and 30 times per day!

We should stop complaining about almost everything that crosses our path, and start being grateful for what we have. Consider the following:

- Before complaining about how lousy your food taste, think of the starving people who have nothing to eat.
- Before complaining about how far you need to walk, think of people in wheelchairs.

- Before complaining about your spouse, think of the lonely people without companions.
- Before complaining about your kids, think of couples who desire to have children but remain barren.
- Before complaining about how small your house is, think of the homeless sleeping on the sidewalk every night.
- Before complaining about how hard your work is, think of the unemployed without income hoping to have your job.

Complaining is counterproductive so you must avoid doing it as much as possible. Life is a gift indeed. You can choose to be happy and make your life more enriching. And you can take proactive steps towards becoming a happier you by complaining less, and taking a more positive outlook in life.

Many people enjoy complaining as much as they enjoy doing nothing about it. It is sad, but this is the true state of affairs. Do you know that the only thing you'll achieve in complaining is convincing others that you are not in control of the situation? That is all complaining does, and nothing worthwhile is ever accomplished. Are you aware that there is always a person somewhere who is happy with less than what you have? Why not just start doing what you love instead of complaining about what you hate? Don't waste another minute of your time whining and complaining. Spend time doing something about it instead. Dale Carnegie said it so well: "Any fool can criticize, condemn, and complain, and most do."

Happiness comes a lot easier when you stop complaining about your problems, and start being grateful for all the problems you don't have. Hence, stop complaining and be grateful, and start living a more meaningful and fruitful life. Take this challenge—try going 24 hours without complaining, not even once, and see the changes in your attitude and perspective of life. Just do it now. And trust me, your life will start changing!

Be More Grateful

A grateful person is a happy person. Even science backs this claim. Scientific research found that people who are grateful:

- are more optimistic
- are less prone to depression
- are more generous and helpful
- are more contented and satisfied with life
- experience less stress
- sleep better
- have more compassion
- have higher levels of vitality and positive emotions
- place less emphasis on materialism
- make better progress towards personal goals
- report fewer physical symptoms and feel healthier
- win new friends and open the door to more relationships

In a world where most of us are programmed to strive for more, and desire what is better, faster and stronger, it becomes easy to forget to appreciate what we do have. To be happier, set aside time to reflect on what we have regularly.

Let me share with you a story...

Joanne is an orphan girl who is blind at birth. Because of the blindness, Joanne hated herself and everybody, except Ben, her loving boyfriend who is always there for her. She complains frequently because she couldn't see and appreciate the things around her. And she told Ben that if she could see one day, she would marry him. Every day, Ben would patiently describe the beautiful things around her so she could feel better.

One day, a call came from a hospital informing Joanne that someone donated a pair of eyes to her, and asked her to come for the eye transplant surgery. Joanne was overjoyed upon hearing the news. The surgery was a success.

When the bandages came off, Joanne could see everything, including her boyfriend who was beside her all the time. Ben then asked her: "Darling, now that you can see, will you marry me?" Joanne saw Ben for the very first time but was shock to discover that he is blind, just like her before.

Disappointed, she responded, "Sorry Ben, I never knew you are blind. I can't marry you because it would really be a burden for me." Ben, utterly heartbroken upon hearing what Joanne had said to him, left in tears. And he never visited Joanne again.

A few days later, Joanne went back to the hospital for a follow-up checkup and the doctor passed her a letter. In it was written: "Darling, I hope you're enjoying the beautiful world around you. Please take good care of yourself and my eyes!" The girl broke down in tears, shocked that Ben would sacrifice his own sight just for her. Though she can now see, she will never see her wonderful boyfriend again.

Stop Comparing Yourself with Others

Comparing yourself with others is one bad habit you must learn to break. This is because making comparisons will only keep you feeling lousy about yourself. When you see what others are doing on social media, on TV, and at work, you start to compare yourself with them. Everybody seem more accomplished, have better job titles, are physically fitter, are richer, and have nicer homes compared to you. Such negative comparisons will make you feel inadequate, stressful, jealous and inferior.

Let's face it. No matter how much you have accomplished in life, there will always be someone out there who is better than you. Whether in your own hometown or in other parts of the world, people who are wealthier, more attractive, and more successful than you will always exist. What can you do about it? Nothing really. Don't you know that even the richest people on the planet have their net worth rankings changed frequently? Check out *The World's Billionaires* list compiled by *Forbes* and see for yourself. Why compare and give yourself the unnecessary stress then?

Making comparisons with others might cause you to make bad judgments and decisions. Break the habit of feeling insecure, envious and discontented with your life as it could set you up for failure ahead. Oscar Wilde said it appropriately: "Be yourself; everyone else is already taken." Stop comparing yourself with others and be your own cheerleader instead.

You Are Unique

No two people in the world are alike—not even twins! Twins, though similar in looks, have very different thinking, personalities and abilities. Even though some people may try to blend in with the majority, that won't make them similar to others. They will remain different no matter how.

We are all created unique and we can't change who we are. We can only change what we do. Everything in life becomes easier once we stop concerning ourselves with what everyone else is doing. Learn to like who we are, and what we are good at. Enjoy being ourselves to make life better, for us and everybody around us. We don't need to fit into a label of who others think we should be. We only need to focus on how we can become the best version of ourselves.

Seek self-improvement rather than to compare yourself with others. Every minute you spend on wishing you had someone else's life is a minute spent wasting your own life. The only person you should try to become better than, is the person you were yesterday. Loving yourself gives you the ability to be in complete control of your life and your happiness.

Don't Envy the Wealthy

It is pointless for anyone to envy the wealthy. Successful people have put in lots of efforts, hard work, and sacrifices to achieve the wealth they are enjoying now. They work hard for their success, which they deserve, and that's fair. Envy is dangerous because it gives birth to hatred. In the same way, all of us have total control of our destinies. We need to have our own ambitions, set our own objectives, and decide how much hard work and sacrifices we are willing to make in order to realize our ambitions.

Whenever I come across any individual who is extremely successful, I would try to find out how that person achieve it, and whether I can too. Never will I be jealous or envious of anyone more successful than me. Being jealous of others when they are rich and successful won't help you in any way. It will only make you a bitter loser. Look at the wealthy with a lens of admiration, and use them as your source of inspiration instead. Learning from successful people is invaluable as they bring a wealth of experience that you can tap into.

Count Your Blessings

Cultivate a habit of gratitude if you want to be wealthy. It may sound strange, but it's true that the more gratitude you feel, the richer you actually are. It is entirely within your control whether you feel poor, rich, or just about fine. There isn't any objective measure of actual richness. You can be having all the money in the world, but still feel you needed more.

The millionaires may be aiming to be billionaires, while the billionaires may still be striving to reach the world's top ten richest list. For us to feel genuinely rich, we need to be grateful for what we already have. Not just the material possessions, but also other things such as family, friends, health, sunshine, rain, clean water, fresh air, being alive, and whatever you can be thankful for.

Let me share with you a secret: The best way to have happy thoughts is by counting your blessings, not counting your money! When you focus on the things you don't have, you tend to forget all the blessings you do have. That's why it's important for you to count your blessings instead of your problems. Moreover, many studies conducted over the past two decades have found that people who consciously count their blessings tend to be happier and less depressed.

Counting our blessings makes us grateful people, which will then lead us to becoming happier people too. Wouldn't this be a good enough reason for us to be grateful in our ultimate pursuit of happiness? If you can't sleep at night due to whatever problems you may be facing, try counting blessings instead of counting sheep!

7

Value Your Greatest Asset

Every day is a bank account, and time is our currency.
No one is rich, no one is poor, we've got 24 hours each.
—Christopher Rice

Imagine a bank account where $86,400 is automatically credited to the account holder at 12:01 a.m. each morning. However, the account carries over no balance and any amount left unused will be removed at exactly 12 midnight every day. What would you do if you own this bank account? You will withdraw every cent in the account every day before midnight without fail, won't you?

The fact is that every one of us owns such a bank account. This bank account is call *time*. Every morning it credits us with 86,400 seconds. Every midnight it writes off the time you failed to invest in a productive way. As this time bank doesn't carry over balances, whatever time that isn't put to good use will be written off as a lost.

Money Can't Buy More Time

Time is a very valuable asset that all of us own. However, it is also a gift to us that most people take for granted. Although time doesn't cost us any money, no amount of money in this world can buy it. You can work hard to earn more money, but you can never buy more time with more money. Moreover, your time living in this world is limited so spend your time wisely.

Don't Let Others Spend Your Time

Very often, the people around you may be guilty of stealing your limited time. If you want to have more precious time to pursue your goals, you must learn to say "no" to your friends or business associates. There are many reasons people say "yes" to invites or any other requests—they don't want to make others feel bad; they don't want to sever current or potential friendships; or they are afraid of being excluded from future possibilities. However, be prepared to piss some people off when you say "no" to them nobody likes being rejected. It's a judgment call you are likely to struggle with.

The truth is, if you need more time to do more productive things, you'll need to say a lot more "no" than "yes" to your inviters. And if you have yet to realize your dream, understand that every time you agree to what others want you to do, you are denying yourself of what you wish to do. Only you can determine how your time will be used. Hence, you need to guard your time or else others will gladly spend it for you.

Possessions Mustn't Be Valued More Than Time

Your most valuable asset shouldn't be your money, car, house, career or business. Rather, you should regard time as priceless. It's important that you value time even more than you value money. If you lose your money, you can always earn it back. But once time is lost, it's gone forever. No amount of money can buy an additional second of time. Time is, therefore, the greatest asset that you possess.

Never waste a single minute of your time and don't let anyone steal away your precious time too. Make sure that your time is not wasted on futile and unimportant things by identifying your priorities, managing distractions, and focusing on getting things done efficiently.

Time is Money

We all know this axiom: Time is money. If we have more time and use it in a productive manner, we will have the opportunity to create more wealth. When time is wasted, money together with the success that could have been achieved, are also wasted.

Successful people are very careful how they use their time. They take extra care to make sure that their time is well spent. The fact is, how you use your time will make a lot of difference in determining whether you will be successful or otherwise. If you won't waste precious time and spend it productively, success will be a step closer.

Create an Extra Day a Week

All of us wish we could have more time for ourselves, don't we? The reality is everyone has just 24 hours a day, not a second more. The majority of people have a five-day work week and working eight hours a day. Many hardworking ones, however, put in even longer hours just to meet the harsh demands of their work environments.

Most people simply have too little time left to spend on themselves and their loved ones. How we wish we could magically turn a seven-day week into an eight-day week! This would then "buy" us more time to do the things we have always wanted. Well, the good news is, there is actually a practical way to create an eight-day week. How? It is very simple—just wake up one hour earlier every day! Doing so consistently each day will give you seven more hours a week, which is about an extra working day. You can then use the extra time to work, read, exercise, date your spouse, play with your kids, meet friends, or do whatever you want. Isn't that wonderful?

Don't Spend Time Oversleeping

The majority of highly successful people wake up early in the morning and start their day before most of us are even awake. By rising early, they have more luxury time to do the things they want and to prepare for the day ahead. They never think of waking up earlier as a punishment. It really isn't. You will get out of bed early every day when you are motivated and purpose-driven; and you will look forward to another brand new day. You are less likely to get distracted and will have more willpower in the early hours than later in the day. Waking up earlier will also allow you to set the tone for a happier and more productive day.

Michelle Gaas (former Starbucks President and current Kohl's CEO) for example, sets her alarm at 4:30 a.m. to go running before she starts work. Tim Cook gets up at an even more ungodly hour than most. As reported by *Inc.*, Cook once told sportscaster Alan Wilkins in a rugby match, "I wake up at 3:45 a.m., I do e-mail at 4:30 a.m., I'm in the gym by 5:00 a.m. And I work straight until eight or nine at night. And then I do it all over again the next day. But I love it, it's my life."

Many people sleep more than necessary, especially during weekends when they don't need to rise early to report for work. I know of people who sleep way past noon during weekends, public holidays and on days they are on leave. They sleep between 12 to 15 hours on non-working days!

I'm not suggesting that you don't get enough sleep from now onwards. And I'm certainly not asking you to sleep only when you're dead! Getting a good night's sleep is no doubt very important for your health and well-being.

Skimping on sleep isn't good for anyone. Getting insufficient sleep constantly not only causes irritability and sluggishness during the day, it might even lead to certain chronic diseases. We need a good night's rest, normally seven to eight hours sleep, for our body to stay in optimal health and function properly. The amount of sleep needed varies from person to person. In general, most experts recommend that healthy adults should get seven to nine hours of sleep every night.

We have to be aware that sleeping too much could be problematic too. In fact, studies have shown that having too much sleep isn't good for our health. Oversleeping is associated with many health issues such as headaches, depression, obesity, heart disease and type 2 diabetes.

People who sleep a lot may also feel or believe there is nothing worth for them to get up for. It has been proven that people who hate their jobs, or don't enjoy what they are doing, tend to oversleep. These are the people who choose sleeping as a route to escape from reality. However, this is certainly not a good solution because the moment they wake up, their problems would still be there. Therefore, action must be taken to get to the root of the problem in order to solve it.

If anyone consistently needs more than nine hours of sleep every night to feel rested, it could be a warning sign of other health-related issues. Seek a doctor for professional advice if the oversleeping persists.

Break the Habit of Waking up Late

If you are trying to break the habit of waking up late, don't try to be too ambitious from the beginning. You'll likely hit the snooze button of your alarm clock just to sleep a little longer should you try to change your late rising habit too drastically. Try to build the habit of rising early slowly instead.

For instance, if you normally wake up at 7:00 a.m. every morning, set your alarm 15 minutes earlier each day, starting at 6:45 a.m. instead of going straight to 5.00 a.m. on the first day. To maintain the sufficient sleep time of seven to eight hours that your body needs, hit the bed 15 minutes earlier every night.

We must all learn to value time more. Do our best not to waste too much time oversleeping and spend more time doing productive things. Imagine tomorrow would be the last day of our life, would we continue to stay in bed? We will remain awake to make the most of our remaining hours in this world, wouldn't we?

Every day should matter because life is made up of days—days like today. So, let's treasure time and jump out of bed early to enjoy every moment of life. Each and every single day of our lives!

8

Dare to Dream Again

The future belongs to those who believe in the beauty of their dreams.
—Eleanor Roosevelt

Your dreams form the foundation of success. Successful people always begin with a dream. They not only dream big dreams, but display great courage to do things that others say can't be done. While achieving your dreams may be challenging, having to deal with setbacks and failures along the way, it's surely worth it. Just look at the happiest and most successful people in the world. They have all achieved their dreams—doing something they love, creating something they believe in, and living a life of purpose and passion. If you're doing that, it doesn't matter anymore how much money you'll be bringing in.

Many people have long forgotten the dreams they used to have when they were kids. As they progress in the journey of life, they are simply too tied up with their daily activities, so much so that they failed to discover what they really want to pursue in life. They constantly find themselves trap in a routine work system that can potentially rob them of their dreams.

Following your dreams is easier said than done. For some people, their dream path might pan out well, but for most of us, the journey to achieving our dreams is long and challenging.

First and foremost, you must start dreaming first before your dreams can come true. Otherwise, you won't be developing your potential to the fullest, and at the same time, ignoring what is truly important in your life. The eight practical steps to take in the pursuit of your dreams are:

1. Learn to Dream

We are born to have dreams. Children often share about their dreams. They tell their parents what they hope to be when they grow up. However, there are times when their parents shrieked, "Stop dreaming and get on with your homework!" Incidents in the classroom where teachers who noticed students dreaming in class and start yelling, "Stop dreaming and pay attention!" are also common. I was being yelled at by my primary school teacher too.

Under such environment where children learn and grow up, dreaming seems to be an unproductive act. Many are told not to dream at a tender age! As individuals grow, they are told to forget their dreams and be pragmatic because they are living in a real world, not a fantasy world. In the end, many of them get realistic and gave up their dreams totally.

2. Dream Big Dreams

All of us dream differently. Never set mental boundaries on what you're capable of achieving. Dreams are free anyway. So long as you dream, you might as well have big dreams. Many times, our dreams are at odds with our realities, demanding freedom and resources that we might not yet have. But this doesn't make our dreams impossible to achieve. A lot of people don't achieve greater success simply because they limit their own beliefs.

Your dreams define you so keep them alive. If you abandon your dreams, what other things could possibly keep you motivated? Don't be ashamed of your dream. You may encounter people mocking you if your dreams are big. Ignore these people because they won't be the ones helping you succeed.

Many people don't always hold tight to their dreams. They give up when they encounter setbacks half way through their journey to realize their goals. The successful ones are those who continue to press on without giving up, no matter what. They remain committed and will do anything to make their dreams a reality.

3. Set Some Goals

Everyone needs a dream and probably have one. There are people who aspire to retire before the age of 50 to travel round the world and enjoy life. Others may just want to buy a beautiful house with a nice swimming pool to go along. Whatever their dreams may be, chances are that most of their dreams will cost money. It is also likely that they don't have the money to fulfill their dreams at the moment. To realize dreams, people will have to set goals and have a money plan.

Goal-setting is about taking your wildest dreams—be they wealth, health, or happiness—and taking steps in the right direction to reach your goals. There is no point taking any step unless you know where you are going. Your dreams have to be clear to you. Before setting your goals, you must know exactly what you hope to achieve. Otherwise, you will be going round in circles. Research has found that gaining more clarity of your dreams and goals are essential so that you will have the motivation to achieve them. If you aren't clear on what you are working towards, it will be difficult for you to remain focus and motivated arising from hazy targets.

4. Write a Dream List

Take one day off and go to a place that won't give you any disturbance. Bring along a writing pad and a pen. If you can, leave your mobile phone at home to free you from any possible interference. Write down a dream list of what you want to have, what you want to be, and what you want to do.

Following are some examples:

- I want to be financially free by 30 years old.
- I want to be a millionaire by 40 years old.
- I want to spend more quality time with my family.
- I want to take family vacations four times a year.
- I want to have $1 million in my bank account in five years.
- I want to buy a bungalow with a pool for my retirement.

Dreams will stay out of reach unless they are unambiguous, tied to goals, and set in motion with a well-defined plan. The dream list, together with the goals you set, must be realistic and achievable. Once you have a set of goals and a plan to accomplish them, your mind would become more focused, and you will be one step closer to achieving your dreams.

5. Take Action Immediately

After writing a dream list with clearly-defined goals, take immediate action to work towards making your dreams come true. Very often, people intend to take action after listing down their dreams when their emotions are still high. However, if they don't translate their intentions into actions soon, their passion will likely diminish over time. Weeks later, the passion will grow cold and then months later, that passion may be gone forever!

There are five birds resting on the fence and a minute later, three birds decide to fly off to search for food. How many birds are left on the fence? Did I hear you say two birds? If so, that is incorrect. There should still be five birds resting on the fence. Why? Because deciding to fly off isn't the same as taking action to fly away. The birds wouldn't be able to get food until they actually fly off from their comfortable resting place.

In pursuing your dreams, don't just think, you need to do. Thinking isn't the same as doing. The doing part is easy. It's the overthinking that makes it hard. The more you think, the more your mind will develop resistance. So, start taking immediate action to make your dreams come true—sooner rather than later.

6. Never Quit

Take courage to pursue your dreams and don't quit. Successful people cling to their dreams against all odds. They pursue their dreams no matter what and how long it takes. You must be mentally prepared that following your dreams can be exhausting and often requires a lot of your energy. You're also likely to meet many obstacles along the way. And it's easy to get discouraged if you only think about the obstacles and challenges before you. You must remain motivated and focus only on your ultimate destination.

You must hang on to your dreams, even in the toughest of circumstances. Rest if you must, but never quit. Perseverance is a quality you're going to need to move closer to fulfilling your dream. It may not be easy though, but trust me, it is definitely worth it. Persistence is what separates the successful from the mere wishful thinkers.

7. Flee from Dream Killers

A group of frogs was travelling through the woods and two of them fell into a deep pit. When the other frogs saw how deep the pit was, they shouted at the two hapless frogs, telling them that they were as good as dead. The two frogs ignored the comments and tried to jump up out of the pit with all their might. The other frogs kept telling them to stop, that they were as good as dead. Finally, one of the frogs got discouraged by what the other frogs were saying and gave up trying. He fell down and died shortly.

The other frog continued to jump as hard as he could. Once again, the crowd of frogs yelled at him to stop the pain and just die. He continued to jump even harder and with one final gigantic leap, he made it out of the pit. Amazed by his seemingly impossible feat, the other frogs asked him, "Did you not hear us?" The frog explained to them that he was deaf and thought they were encouraging him and cheering him on the entire time!

Dream killers are devastating to your success. It pays to turn a deaf ear to the multitude of discouraging comments and noises around us. Your friends, colleagues and even your loved ones could possibly be one of your dream killers. There will be enough people out there who will try to distract you, confuse you, or persuade you to build the life they want, not the life that you want.

Stop listening to people who tell you why you wouldn't achieve your dreams. You just need to believe you can achieve whatever you set out to do. Ignore anyone who tries to tell you what to think or do. Follow your own instincts and goals instead. Always remember that other people can only discourage you temporarily, but you're the only one who can stop yourself from being discouraged permanently.

8. Stop Giving Excuses

Have you realized that children frequently talk about what they can do whereas many adults are doing just the opposite? Very often, adults talk about what they can't do, and provide reasons to justify. Stop giving reasons why you can't achieve your dreams. Many of these so-called reasons are merely excuses. If you keep giving excuses for not achieving, it wouldn't take long before you successfully convince yourself that your dreams are out of reach.

Life can be a self-fulfilling prophecy. Your dreams today can create the life you live tomorrow. As Henry Ford rightly puts it: "Whether you think you can or cannot, you're absolutely right." How true are his wise words!

There are no whys or maybes. While there is a time to ask questions, there is also a time to stop asking and do the necessary. Don't be pushed by your problems; be led by your dreams instead. Stop giving yourself excuses. Now's the time to just do it and realize your dreams!

PART TWO

GET RICH

Fortune sides with him who dares.
—Virgil

My financial situation in the 1990s wasn't all that rosy. I was nowhere near being rich even though I was earning a five-figure monthly salary in the late 1990's. And I frequently had sleepless nights worrying about money. Why? Because I had an ever-growing mountain of debt! I was lacking in financial literacy and I wasn't managing my money well at that time.

Fast forward to today, I now enjoy the money that comes from my investments, and I spend time doing the things I'm passionate about. It took me many years and a ton of hard work before I finally become financially free, and wealthy at the same time. My money mindset and habits have changed dramatically in the process of increasing my financial IQ and becoming investment-savvy.

You won't be waking up one day and find yourself becoming rich in an instance. Building wealth takes time. Most wealthy individuals didn't get rich quickly, and it can be a long journey for some.

The first $1 million is often the hardest and takes the longest time to achieve for most millionaires. It took me nearly 16 years (from the day I started working after graduating from university) to achieve my first million dollars. My second million dollars was achieved much faster, around four years after earning my first million, as my income increases substantially arising from my growing investments. Subsequent millions are made even quicker as I gained investing experience coupled with more capital to finance bigger investments.

Don't think of wealth creation in a complex way. Getting rich isn't complicated; it really shouldn't be. You just need to follow a three-step process to build wealth:

1. Sell your time for money (that means working at the job for income).
2. Spend less than you earn and save the rest (also known as living a frugal life).
3. Invest your savings to make more money (buy income producing assets).

Just keep repeating the three steps listed above and you will be on your way to achieving massive wealth over time. Getting wealthy is really that simple. However, it is certainly not easy because your mindset, habits, attitudes, and the way you live your life has to change accordingly. These are choices you make if you wish to be rich one day. You are only constrained by how much time you have in this world to learn and invest. Other than that, the sky is the limit to how much wealth you wish to amass.

9

Where Are You Financially?

When your self-worth goes up, your net worth goes up with it.
—Mark Victor Hansen

To start your wealth journey, you have to know where to begin from. Even with a map in your hand, you can't reach any destination if you don't know where your location is. Your financial journey is no different. You must first know where you are financially before you can reach your desired financial destination. In other words, you need to know your net worth. It's an important starting point on your financial map.

Wealthy people know their net worth whereas poor people couldn't be bothered. In my interactions with friends and business associates, I found that many of them don't know exactly how much they are worth. They have actually lost track of how much they own and how much they owe. And that is a pretty dangerous position to be in.

Do You Know Where Are You Now?

Many people have no idea where they are heading financially, particularly for those with high debt levels. People who owe a lot of money might be tempted to think that if they avoid looking at their dismay financial standings, their debts would fade away. Sorry to disappoint, but that won't happen. We should never behave like ostriches, hiding our heads below the ground, and be oblivious of the problems around us. If we want to improve our financial situations, we need to know exactly where we are now, and then start taking actions to improve the financials.

No matter how you feel about your debts, you need to get the facts right and up to date to keep your financial house in order. Don't put it off to another day because it won't get any easier. In order to be ahead in your finances, you must get organized and determine your net worth. If you have not already done so, do it as soon as you possibly can.

Determine Your Net Worth

Calculating your personal net worth is important because it can provide a snapshot of your financial situation at this point in time. Your net worth, in simple terms, is the difference between what you *own* and what you *owe*. In other words, it is the grand total of your assets minus your liabilities.

Once you get your net worth statement up, it becomes a useful tool to help you measure your financial progress. The net worth figure can help deliver a wake-up call if you are completely off track, or offer a "job-well-done" confirmation. When calculated periodically, your net worth can be regarded as a financial report card that allows you to evaluate your current financial health and can help you figure out what needs to be done to achieve your financial goals.

To determine your net worth, you will need all the financial information concerning the things that you own and the debts that you owe. When you get organized and complete the net worth statement for the first time, subsequent recordings would be a breeze. I suggest you do this at the comfort of your home because you would need easy access to all the necessary financial statements and other details. Most people would have these things kept in their own homes.

WHERE ARE YOU FINANCIALLY?

Ready to start? If so, go grab a pen and some blank papers now. You can use the following worksheet as a guide.

NET WORTH STATEMENT	
ASSETS	
Cash and Bank Accounts:	**Amount**
Cash	
Savings accounts	
Current accounts	
Term deposits	
Others	
Investments:	
Stocks / Bonds / Unit trusts / REITS / Gold	
Properties (Investment)	
Insurance (cash value)	
Other assets:	
House (own stay)	
Car	
Jewelleries / Antiques / Collectibles	
Retirement accounts:	
Retirement plans	
Other retirement funds	
Total Assets	
LIABILITIES	
Property loans	
Car loans	
Credit card balances	
Other loans	
Total Liabilities	
NET WORTH (Total Assets less Total Liabilities)	

List down the market value of your assets (the things you own) which include:

- Cash and bank accounts (cash in hand, savings accounts, current accounts, certificate of deposit, term deposits, digital currencies).
- Investments (stocks, bonds, unit trusts, REITs (real estate investment trusts), investment properties, gold certificates, gold bars and coins).
- Insurance (whole life, endowment).
- Other assets (house, car, jewelries, antiques, collectibles).

- Retirement accounts (various retirement plans from around the world depending on your citizenship. For example, in the United States: IRA (Individual Retirement Account), 401(k); in Singapore: CPF (Central Providence Funds); in Malaysia: EPA (Employees Provident Fund); or any other type of retirement plans in your country of residence).

To simplify the process, you may want to exclude items of smaller value such as furniture, TV, audio system, refrigerator, washing machine, and the like. Similarly, you need not include personal items like your handbags (unless you own a $200,000 Hermès Birkin crocodile skin handbag) or watches (unless your collection includes a Patek Philippe and other luxury watches).

When you are done recording your assets, move on to list down your liabilities (the debts you owe) including housing loans, car loans, personal loans, hire purchase loans, bank overdrafts, credit card balances, and any other loans.

Amend the details in the worksheet in accordance to your current needs. Once all the figures for your assets and liabilities are written down, you can transfer all the data into the net worth statement worksheet to calculate your personal net worth.

After this exercise, I hope your net worth will turn out to be positive where you own more assets than liabilities. Otherwise, start planning immediately to get your finances back on track. To improve your net worth, you will have to work towards increasing your income (or assets) and decreasing your debts (or liabilities).

Your net worth should be used to track your financial progress from year to year. Do this exercise once a year and continually work towards growing your net worth. Keep your finances in order starting today, and you shall certainly be reaping great dividends in the years ahead!

10

Invest in Yourself

*Invest in as much of yourself as you can,
you are your own biggest asset by far.*
—Warren Buffett

Attaining financial success requires plenty of education to improve your financial intelligence. You must read a lot of books, magazines and articles on personal finance; learn from industry leaders to be money-savvy; and keep up to date with relevant and recent news. Investing in yourself gives you the boost you need to succeed. You become the best instrument for success as you acquire the essential knowledge and skills needed to build wealth.

Wealth is the greatest weapon against poverty. And to build wealth to fight poverty, understanding and applying the principles of wealth is the key. The fact is, the best investment anyone can make isn't term deposits, bonds, stocks, mutual funds, gold coins, commodities, or even properties—it is personal development. Can you think of another better tool to create wealth other than yourself? Anyone can take away the wealth of a successful individual, but that person can simply make money and accumulate wealth again with knowledge and investing skills. However, nobody can ever take knowledge away from you—it will remain with you now, and always.

Money Doesn't Solve Money Problems

Money isn't the answer to money woes. The job promotion that comes with a good pay raise you've been wanting isn't going to solve your financial troubles. If you're faced with a mountain of debt, and experiencing a hard time paying your bills arising from bad money habits, having more money isn't the solution. Why? Because in the same spirit of the principle called Parkinson's Law (where work expands to fill the time available for its completion), your higher income will also be met by rising expenses.

There are instances where having excess cash can exacerbates money problems. We have seen lottery winners receiving millions of dollars only to lose it all within a few years. There are also some professional athletes who made millions during their prime years but end up broke after retiring from their professions. It may be incomprehensible but there are many people who just can't handle a sudden windfall of wealth.

So, what is the cure for money problems? I believe financial literacy is the answer. It is the understanding of how money works that will solve money issues, not money itself. All financial struggles—getting into debt, difficulty paying off debts, compulsive spending, and having no savings—are mostly due to a person's behavior, and him not knowing how to handle money. The good news is you are in total control of your financial situation. You can choose to improve your financial literacy and be the cure of your own money behavioral problems. Reading this book is already a good start. Keep the development of your financial intelligence in progress; manage your money wisely; and you will overcome your financial stress and improve your finances in due time.

Knowledge Is the Best Investment

Benjamin Franklin nailed it perfectly: "An investment in knowledge pays the best interest." Knowledge plays a part in everything you do—it can help you do your job better, make wiser decisions, invest profitably, sell more products, enjoy greater health, play sports better, and the list goes on and on. Franklin understood the value of chasing after knowledge and learning without stopping, as confirmed by the genius Albert Einstein who once said, "Once you stop learning, you start dying." No wonder successful people are always reading, learning and developing themselves on a regular basis.

The great entrepreneur and motivation speaker, Jim Rohn, said, "Formal education will make you a living; self-education will make you a fortune." Yet, many people behave as though their learning journeys end the moment they finished high school or graduated from university. They stop acquiring new knowledge, follow the conventional path of seeking a career, and move with the herds till the day they retire. This way of living life is wrong, especially in today's economy where change is the new constant. They ignored the fact that the more you learn, the more you will earn. That is why many people remain stuck in the rat race and finding it difficult to set themselves free. It is certainly possible to escape the rat race. You just need to have the financial knowledge to help you make the right investment decisions. Once you achieved financial freedom, you can have the immediate option to get out of the rat race if you choose to. I did it. And you can too.

Increase Your Financial Intelligence

Would you drive your kids to school if you have not taken any lessons in driving? Or would you jump into the deep sea if you have not learned how to swim? I'm certain you wouldn't. I surely wouldn't too. Yet, millions of people everywhere are doing something just as inconceivable—they go through life without learning about personal finance. Managing money is an important aspect of a person's life. How can anyone play and score well in the game of wealth without understanding its rules?

Personal finance is an overlooked area in our educational system. It is never taught in schools. In my opinion, money management skills should be taught to children at an early age.

People are struggling with their finances because they never learn how to manage money wisely in schools. And most parents are incapable of teaching their children money management skill. It is our responsibility to ensure that our finances are handled well. At the moment, financial literacy is sorely lacking everywhere.

Many people don't spend much time learning or understanding the details before they buy things like properties, cars, or financial products such as bonds, stocks, mutual funds, and so on. They have little or no knowledge about what they are doing with their money. On the contrary, people tend to put in more effort when it comes to spending money on lifestyle and entertainment. They bother to research extensively for good restaurants to eat or where to go for their holidays. But, when it comes to buying a big-ticket item like a house, which is probably their most expensive purchase in their lifetime, many depend solely on the recommendations of their real estate agents. They don't ensure if they are getting the best deal for the house, or whether they are indeed buying the right property given their current financial status and commitments.

Most people rather spend money instead of investing it. They spend most of what they earn, with some even spending more than they earn using credit to facilitate their never-dying hunger to enjoy life. In terms of time, they spend it with people they don't really like, doing things they don't enjoy, and then waking up one day wondering why their life is the way it is. Is it a mystery why people lose money in investments or find it hard to become rich in their lifetime?

Successful people choose to invest their money and time wisely. They see life through a lens of investment. The wealthy invest their money in creating additional revenue streams and mostly avoiding buying depreciating assets or any other liabilities. They are very conscious of how they spend their time. They invest time to achieve their goals. Wealthy people invest in themselves by reading books, attending seminars, and taking courses that will help them further their interests. They understand that knowledge is vital to their success, and that ignorance is extremely costly.

They spend money and time to improve their financial IQ, knowing that it would have cost them their financial success should they not do so.

Develop a Good Reading Habit

The road to knowledge is paved with books. While there may be different roads leading to success, many of the world's famous movers and shakers have attributed their success to an insatiable reading habit. These business leaders are selective about what they read. They often look to satisfy their hunger for knowledge opting to be educated rather than to be entertained.

Even the billionaires don't take short cuts for their rise to the upper echelons of the business world. They invest their time into a simple habit that will help them outperform competitors—reading. In fact, most successful people credit reading as a major factor in their success. This is certainly one of the good habits we can pick up from the best of the best. Let's take a look at four billionaires and examine their reading habits.

1. Warren Buffett

Warren Buffett, CEO of Berkshire Hathaway, reportedly spends five to six hours reading five different newspapers every day—*Forbes*, *The Financial Times*, *The New York Times*, *The Wall Street Journal* and *USA Today*. At the age of 19, he picked up a copy of Benjamin Graham's book, *The Intelligent Investor*, to read. The book has helped shaped Buffett's investment philosophy after he read it. And the rest is history.

Responding to a question about how to prepare for an investing career during an investing class at Columbia University in 2000, Buffett told the class of 166 students, "Read 500 pages like this every day" while reaching toward a stack of manuals and papers. He continued, "That's how knowledge works. It builds up like compound interest. All of you can do it, but I guarantee not many of you will do it."

To this day, Buffett still spend as much as 80% of his day reading and credits many of his great money decisions to his voracious reading habit. "I read and think," Buffett once said. "So, I do more reading and thinking, and make less impulse decisions than most people in business. I do it because I like this kind of life." The business tycoon reads widely not because he has to, but because he loves to.

2. Bill Gates

Bill Gates, the principal founder of Microsoft Corporation, has attested to reading 50 books a year, which works out to be about one book per week. Gates loves reading books so much as a child that his parents ended up making a new rule that no books are allowed at the dinner table.

The majority of the books he reads are nonfiction dealing with public health, disease, engineering, business, and science. Gates reads a novel once in a while though. As one of the founding fathers of technology, it may surprise many that he still prefers reading a book the old-fashioned way. And writing notes in the margins of the book is one habit he finds difficult to break.

You might want to check out his personal blog, *GatesNotes*, which features a wide selection of books that Gates recommends.

3. Mark Zuckerberg

Embarking on a mission to connect people around the world, Mark Zuckerberg, founder and CEO of Facebook, announced on his page in 2015 that his resolution for the year would be to read a new book every other week; not just books about business or technology, but with an emphasis on learning about different beliefs, cultures and technologies. He then started a book club and created a Facebook page called *A Year of Books* and urged his friends to join him in the project.

Zuckerberg wrote on his page, "I've found reading books very intellectually fulfilling. Books allow you to fully explore a topic and immerse yourself in a deeper way than most media today. I'm looking forward to shifting more of my media diet towards reading books."

4. Mark Cuban

Mark Cuban, owner of Dallas Mavericks of the National Basketball Association (NBA), is a vocal supporter of treating business like a sport. Cuban credits much of his success to his reading habit. Being a voracious reader, Cuban reads excessively for new ideas. He looks for competitive edge by reading more than 3 hours almost every day, just to learn more about the industries he works in. Cuban said that this reading routine has worked wonders at the start of his career. "Everything I read was public," he wrote in his blog. "Anyone could buy the same books and magazines. The same information was available to anyone who wanted it. Turns out most people didn't want it."

Never Stop Learning

Abraham Lincoln, one of the greatest presidents in U.S. history, once said, "I do not think much of a man who is not wiser today than he was yesterday." The investment you make in yourself will always pay off. The wiser you are, the better the decisions you will make.

In terms of knowledge, if you are not getting better today, you are getting worst tomorrow. That is because new ideas, new technologies, new discoveries, and thereby new knowledge, keep coming up in a fast-changing world. It pays to make it a point to always keep improving yourself each day by learning new things. Longtime wealthy individuals know that to remain relevant in their field, they must continue learning and adapting. They stay updated on world news and read books regularly to expand their knowledge as well as keep them inspired.

Learning is a continuous journey. It isn't something that should stop. Your education should be a work-in-progress till the day you pass on. You need to be putting money into yourself if you want to succeed. This means spending money on things that would equip you to be the best at what you do. Every time you read a book, attend a seminar, or participate in a workshop, you will be walking away with something that no one can take from you—that something is knowledge. Knowledge makes you a better person and allows you to be an expert in a particular field. Competition can't take it from you, and surely the government can't tax your knowledge and expertise.

Investing in knowledge makes the best investment because the price of ignorance is costly. Start taking action to improve your knowledge and learn about how to get better at what you're doing. Establish a reading routine by allocating some time for reading each day. Read books, biographies, newspapers, magazines, and other articles daily for at least an hour a day. Listen to audio books, podcasts and interviews. Observe and study what other successful people are doing to make them who they are today. Knowledge is what separates you from the herd. Don't stop learning.

11

Create a Budget

*A budget is telling your money where to go
instead of wondering where it went.*
—John C. Maxwell

Budget Planning

Planning a budget is necessary at the country level down to the individual level. Governments must have a budget so that leaders are held accountable. Corporations and businesses need a budget so as to ensure expenses do not exceed revenues. We need a budget for the same reasons. To be good financial stewards, we need to be accountable for our money and ensure our spending won't exceed our income. Proper money management requires us to track our money movements. The reason for managing our finances well is obvious—we can get richer when we gain proper control of our money.

Some of us may not be fascinated by the term budget. It just sounds too serious, unexciting and even intimidating. Many people think of budgeting as a restrictive loss of freedom to spend their money. They are also afraid that doing up a budget requires never-ending and boring accounting entries that takes up many hours of their time. It's actually untrue. Budgeting is simple. So, let's just think of a budget simply as a spending and saving plan. This makes it sounds as though a lot less work is involved. You just need to draw out a plan for spending and saving your money, nothing complicated at all. It's also important to make your budget realistic because if it isn't, you'll likely not stick to it.

Setting Up a Budget

A budget is simply a spending plan that takes into account both current and future income and expenses. The importance of creating a budget can't be overemphasized. Without a budget, you might run out of money before your next paycheck. So, if you want to have financial security, adhering to a budget that you have created is the way to go.

There are many benefits of setting up a budget. A budget helps you meet your saving targets, reveals whether you are living within your means, and forces you to distinguish between needs and wants. Creating a budget that you have control over lets you make better financial decisions by removing unnecessary expenditures, and allows you to focus on your money goals. A budget, therefore, lets you tell your money where you want it to go instead of having you wondering where your money went. It will also enable you to plan the way you use your money so you can achieve your objectives as well as your purpose in life.

The best way to set up a budget is to calculate your monthly income and determine your monthly expenses. If you are currently in debt, put in the amounts you pay every month to service your debts. Allocate the amount of money you feel you need for entertainment, holidays and other variable expenses. Keep such expenses low—and religiously stick to it—especially if you still have outstanding consumer debts such as credit card balances.

CREATE A BUDGET

Following is a basic budget worksheet that you could use to plan your monthly budget.

MONTHLY BUDGET WORKSHEET			
Income		**Amount**	
Salary			
Investment Income			
Others			
	Total Income		
Expenses	**Budget Amount**	**Actual Amount**	**Difference**
Mortgage / Rent			
Property tax			
Utilities (electricity, water, gas)			
Telephone (fixed line, mobile line)			
Cable TV / Internet			
Car loan			
Motor insurance			
Car maintenance			
Petrol / Parking / Toll			
Groceries			
Food (restaurants, fast food, etc.)			
Insurance premium			
Credit card payment			
Entertainment			
Vacation			
Others			
	Total Expenses		
Surplus / Deficit (*Total Income less Total Expenses*)			

Feel free to make amendments to the budget worksheet as every individual's financial situation is different, and adjust to cater to your own income or spending. Provide an estimate of what you have in each category to prevent you from overspending.

A monthly budget is generally the most reasonable timeframe for any personal or household budget. However, there could be income sources and expenses that may not follow a monthly schedule perfectly. For example, there are certain dividend-paying stocks which pay cash dividends on a quarterly or half-yearly basis. There are also people who receive weekly salaries or wages. Some pay their recurring insurance premiums annually. Just multiply or divide the amount accordingly to get the monthly income or expenses in such cases.

Track Your Expenses and Amend Budget If Necessary

After creating your budget, take a few minutes every day to keep track of your expenses in each category. Tracking your expenses each day will allow you to know when to stop spending, especially when you are about to exceed your budgeted amount. You can make adjustments throughout the month if it is necessary to do so. For example, you may need to send your car to the workshop for repair, and wish to move your money from the entertainment category to help cover the repair cost.

After a month, see whether your budget needs adjustments. For instance, you may find that you could cut back spending in some areas, while requiring more money in others. If you have surplus money at the end of the month, put it into your savings account for future investments. When deficit occurs, you must cut back on your spending. If you still have deficits after cutting back on your expenses significantly, you'll have to quickly find ways to increase your income—ask for a pay rise, do some freelance work, give tuition during weekends, or look for a better paying job elsewhere.

Make it a habit to evaluate your budget at the end of each month. This will help you adjust your spending as you progress forward in life. Keep tweaking your budget until it works well for you. Without a doubt, while a budget would tell you what you can and can't afford, it doesn't have the power to stop you from spending. Therefore, you need to exercise discipline and be committed to stick to the budget that you have put in place. Exercise self-control and avoid careless spending at all cost.

Planning a budget and setting it up is the best way to help you stay on top of your finances—by making sure your money goes where you want it to. Don't view the budget as depriving yourself, but rather, see it as putting yourself in total control of your finances.

12

Keep a Part of All You Earn

*Save a part of your income and begin now,
for the man with a surplus controls circumstances
and the man without a surplus is controlled by circumstances.*
—Henry Buckley

"A part of all you earn is yours to keep" is a basic principle in building wealth taken from *The Richest Man in Babylon*, a book written in the 1920s by George S. Clason. This advice simply suggest you keep aside a portion of your income before you spend it. People who don't adhere to this basic rule will likely end up having not much money remaining.

Pay Yourself First

"Paying yourself first" is a modern financial catchphrase we commonly come across in personal finance literature. It means saving before you do anything else. You'll be setting aside a specific amount of money to be saved upon receiving your paycheck or any other income.

In other words, paying yourself even before you spend any money on your living expenses and making any other discretionary purchases. It's the single best way to save money. This saving method has been proven over time to cause people to change their spending behavior.

As mentioned earlier, this precept has been around for many decades since the book *The Richest Man in Babylon* gives insights on how to save, invest and create wealth. The powerful insights are presented by way of parables. The book tells us about a rich man named Arkad, who despite not having any family wealth or special talents, was known to be the wealthiest man in Babylon.

In one of the parables, the people around Arkad wanted to understand how he had become so successful, and they went to ask him. Arkad responded by telling them how he had enough sense to know that he didn't know everything, and that in order to become wealthy, he would need to ask someone who was wealthy what their secret was. When he found the opportunity one day, he asked a money lender who came to the hall of records where he worked. The money lender told Arkad, "I found the road to wealth when I decided that a part of all I earned was mine to keep. And so will you."

You probably think that everything you earn is yours to keep. However, you have many things to pay in your everyday life— you need to buy food, pay mortgage or rent, pay utility bills, buy clothes, pay for entertainments, pay taxes, and so on. Can you see that much of what you earn isn't yours to keep because a sizable portion would end up in other people's hands? Therefore, if you want to be wealthy, make it a habit to pay yourself first. If you don't, your income will quickly disappear, and none of what you earn will be yours to keep.

Of course, there will be people getting rich in other ways— like marrying the rich, winning the lottery, inheriting riches, or even suing others to get more money. These could be easier paths to riches, but they are the exception rather than the norm. For the rest of us, it would be difficult to get rich until we choose to pay ourselves first.

Most People Pay Others First

The majority of people pay everyone else first for every dollar they earned. They pay the government, banks, credit card companies, telecommunication companies, hotels, restaurants, airlines, and the list continues. It is likely that by the time consumers have paid for everything else, they would have left with little or no money to save—not until the next paycheck arrives. And the cycle continues on and on, month after month, without any substantial amount of money being saved. That is paying yourself last.

People with uncontrollable overspending habits mostly end up owing banks and credit card companies instead. The situation becomes worst when they rollover their credit card debts which carry exorbitant interest rates. If all these circumstances sound all too familiar, then you don't have the habit of paying yourself first.

What About Outstanding Loans?

If you still have consumer debt like credit card debt or other personal loans, clear these outstanding loans first before you start saving. This is because the interest charges are much higher than the interests you earn from your savings.

After clearing your consumer debt, set aside at least 20% of your income for savings. If making a 20% contribution to savings is hard to achieve at the beginning, go for 10% instead; or even 5% if you are still finding it difficult to save 10% of your income. Any amount of monthly savings is clearly better than none at all. Once you are financially more comfortable, gradually increase the amount to save to the targeted twenty percent so that you can achieve a meaningful sum of money for investing purposes later.

The goal of paying yourself first is to help make sure your future financial goals—building up an emergency fund for sudden unexpected expenses; contributing to a retirement fund; saving for long-term goals such as down payment for house, car, etc.; and saving for your retirement—are taken care of. It is important to have these covered before you spend any portion of your paycheck.

It is entirely possible for many to have millions of dollars flowing through their banks in their lifetime. Assuming an individual makes averagely $50,000 per year and working for 45 years before retiring, he or she would have earned $2.25 million! You may not have total control of more than a third of the income you earned due to various expenditures. However, your saving, spending and investing choices in the course of your lifetime would definitely have a major impact on your financial future.

Most People Aren't Saving Enough for Retirement

When it comes to retirement, many people would dream of having a house by the seaside, travelling round the world, and spending quality time with family and friends. Although it's fair enough for anyone to have such wonderful retirement dreams, all of that requires the kind of money most people don't have, or at least yet to have.

To understand whether anyone could afford a comfortable retirement, we just need to take a peek at the amount of money people have in their savings account.

How much money do Americans save? The following statistics and information, provided by GOBankingRates for surveys conducted in 2017 with more than 8,000 Americans, would shed some light.

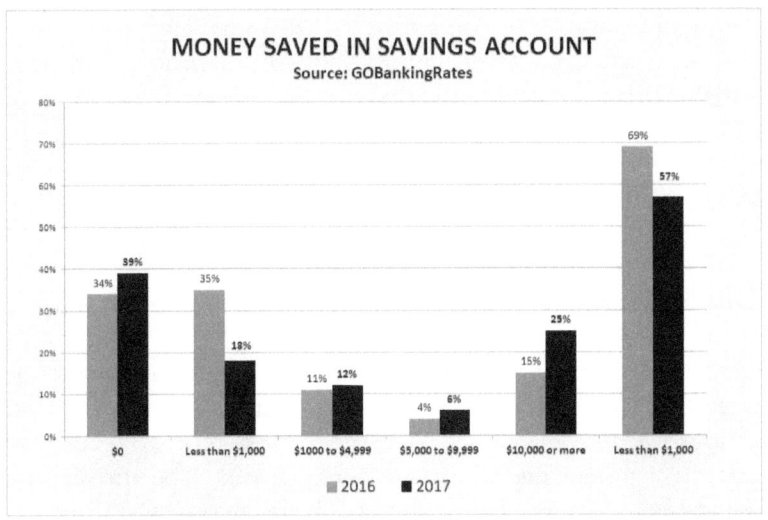

The savings account balances are telling. As can be seen above, more than half of Americans (57%) have less than $1,000 in their savings accounts. Out of this 57%, only 18% have savings up to $999 while the rest, a whopping 39%, have none! Do you think such a situation represent a bright financial future for most people? Unfortunately not.

While there is an improvement from 2016 where 69% of Americans had less than $1,000 in savings (an improvement from 57% the previous year), there are more people (an increase of 5% from the previous year) having no savings at all, up from 34% in 2016 to 39% in 2017. Only a quarter of Americans have $10,000 or more savings. The table below shows the breakdown of the 8,000 plus American respondents for the 2017 survey:

Money saved in the savings account	
$0	39%
Less than $1,000	18%
$1000 to $4,999	12%
$5,000 to $9,999	6%
$10,000 or more	25%

To summarize, more than a third of Americans have zero savings, about a third have less than $5,000 savings, while only a quarter of them have $10,000 or more savings. Not a good overall picture actually. Many Americans could potentially retire broke because they lag behind on savings. Furthermore, financial hardships could occur should there be any emergencies or loss of jobs. There is clearly insufficient savings in most households. For those without much savings, take immediate steps to start saving; not next month, next week, or next time, but today!

How Much Money Should You Set Aside for Retirement?

The amount of money you should save for retirement will be based on your income, your planned retirement age, and the kind of lifestyle you desire to have when you retire. Hence, the retirement money needed is very personal and a specific amount would be arbitrary. Cash savings, term deposits, retirement account contributions, and money that you have invested elsewhere will be included as part of your retirement savings.

The following table shows a simple assessment guideline to see if you're setting aside enough savings for your retirement. You should have at least the amount of money saved going by the various age categories.

Ideal Savings for Retirement (assuming $50,000 per year income)		
Age	Target	Amount
In your 20s	25% of annual income	$12,500
By age 30	100% of annual income	$50,000
By age 35	2 times annual income	$100,000
By age 40	3 times annual income	$150,000
By age 45	4 times annual income	$200,000
By age 50	5 times annual income	$250,000
By age 55	6 times annual income	$300,000
By age 60	7 times annual income	$350,000
By age 65	8 times annual income	$400,000
By age 70	9 times annual income	$450,000
By age 75	10 times annual income	$500,000
By age 80	11 times annual income	$550,000

The amount of money listed in the table above could look like a daunting task, but if you put your money to work by investing early in your life, it is not that hard to achieve that kind of savings.

When Should You Start Saving for Retirement?

When it comes to saving for retirement, the early bird gets the worm. The sooner you start saving, the longer the time you have for your money to grow. Hence, the best time for you to start saving for retirement is when you're in your 20s. You only need to save a few thousand dollars a year until you reach retirement age of 65.

For example, if you save $4,500 a year for 45 years starting at age 20, and with an investment return of 6%, you'll get $1 million by the time you retire at the age of 65. Even if you are not in your 20s, it is never too late to start saving money. You just have to save more each year. Assuming the same rate of return of 6%, if you are 30 years old, you will have to save $8,500 a year to get about $1 million at 65 years old. At 40 years old, you will need to save $17,000 a year. And if you start at age 50, you must save $39,000 a year to have $1 million for your retirement at 65.

13

Avoid the Debt Trap

*Debt is like any other trap, easy enough to get into,
but hard enough to get out of.*
—Josh Billings

"A man in debt is so far a slave," said Ralph Waldo Emerson, an American lecturer and philosopher. His words still hold true more than a hundred years later. So many people are enslaved by mounting debts that are suffocating their financial health. Nothing in this world can derail an individual's financial success as effectively as debt.

Today, debt has become a fact of life for many people all over the world. It's the way people pay for just about everything, from big-ticket items such as condominiums and cars, to daily purchases like petrol and potato chips. Although getting into debt isn't always a bad thing (especially when using debt to finance an investment), we should always resist the temptation of getting into debt to purchase things for pure consumption.

Debt drains us financially, emotionally, psychologically and spiritually. Please note that when I talk about debt here, I'm referring to consumer debt, not debt taken up for investing purposes. Incurring debt for the purpose of acquiring an asset that yields good returns, along with sufficient profits to cover the debt repayment, is a different story altogether. There is good debt, and bad debt as well. We shall look at the difference between the two in greater details in a while.

The most common types of debt are loans such as mortgages, car loans, and credit card debt. Staying out of debt seems easy and straightforward. In reality however, millions of debt-ridden people will attest that getting out of debt is much more complicated than that. Blame the billions of dollars spent by companies putting out endless media advertisements that seek to glorify a lavish lifestyle. These advertisements exert great influence on people's belief systems, tastes for finer things in life, and subsequent spending habits, making it even easier for excessive spenders to slide into crushing debts.

The Difference Between Good Debt and Bad Debt

Very few people earn enough money to pay for everything using cash, especially for expensive things like house, car and college education. While it's still possible for anyone to live completely debt-free, it's not necessarily smart in terms of maximizing profits. Hence, the most important consideration when taking out a loan is to determine whether the debt incurred is good or bad. Let's examine the difference between good debt and bad debt.

1. Good Debt

Is there such a thing as good debt? Well, it depends. Generally, a good debt is an investment debt that helps you buy an asset that appreciates in value over time. Your net worth will increase as a result from taking on that debt. Loans for investment properties that will generate rental income, loans for business startups, or student loans for further education, can all be considered good debts. Simply put, good debt helps you build wealth or increases your prospects to become richer in due time.

As all investments carry some degree of risks, take on good debt only if you can afford to pay the loan installments regardless of economic conditions. For example, there are many property investors who struggle financially when their decreasing rental income during economic downturns couldn't cover the loan repayments. Some even have their properties repossessed by banks when they couldn't pay the mortgage loan. These investors shouldn't have incurred the debts in the first place, even if they are used for investments. That is because they don't possess financial holding power to hang on to their properties to withstand cyclical recessions, and to allow those properties to appreciate in value over the long term.

Hence, you must do your sums carefully and consider all scenarios before taking up any debt, even if the debt is deemed to be good.

2. Bad Debt

Bad debt costs you money without improving your financial position. It is the debt incurred to buy unnecessary things that you can't afford to pay upfront. Bad debt buys you liabilities. Things like cars, designer clothes and gadgets are considered liabilities because these things decrease in value over time. Debt on anything that depreciates in value is disastrous!

Motor vehicle loans, payday loans and credit card balances are considered bad debts. In comparison to other types of debt, credit card debt is the worst since banks and credit card companies charge the highest interest rates. Bad debt keeps you poor.

Managing Debt

It is difficult to live completely debt-free because most people won't be able to pay cash upfront for their houses, vehicles or children's tertiary educations. The challenge is to determine which debt makes sense and which doesn't. When the debt does make sense, take the loan only if you are able to pay the monthly installments comfortably.

Ideally, your total debt obligations each month shouldn't exceed 30% of your gross monthly income, or 35% at the very most. However, the reasonable amount of debt you should carry would greatly depend on the stage of life you are at, your financial obligations, and the stability of your job.

Manage your finances wisely by incurring good debt, and reducing or eliminating bad debt. At the end of the day, you just need to have a sense that more income and less debt are both good things.

Debt Addiction

People get themselves into crumbling debts because they lack the discipline to track their finances. Ask any of these debt-ridden people at any time and they're likely clueless of their current financial standing—how much money they have, how much they spend, and the loans they have remaining.

I reckon there are times where debts result from cataclysmic events, emergencies or unexpected situations like seeking emergency treatment at the hospital. But most of the time, financial woes are caused by people's addiction to spending on luxury things that are beyond their means. Please don't get me wrong. I enjoy luxuries as much as the next person. However, the luxury items that I own were all paid in cash, not financed with borrowed money. I'll never incur debt that I can't afford to pay. The problem arises when people let their debts get out of hand by overspending on non-essential items.

Are you addicted to spending? Find out if the following applies to you:

- Is your debt affecting your reputation?
- Is your debt causing you to have sleepless nights frequently?
- Are you getting drunk frequently due to the high pressure of your debt?

- Are you constantly worrying about losing your job because of high debt?
- Are you fearful that your employer or friends will find out about your debt situation?
- Is your debt situation causing arguments and unhappiness among family members?
- Have you provided false information to have your credit facility or loans approved?
- Have you obtained a loan without giving much thoughts on the interest rate?
- Have you tried to justify debt by believing your job promotion is coming so you will be having more money to pay your debt?

If you can identify with some of the scenarios above, you are likely to be a compulsive spender with a debt that is too high for comfort. In such situation, take immediate action to get out of your debt problems. Don't fall into the debt trap just to keep up with the Joneses. In reality, the Joneses are broke! It is definitely not worth letting unnecessary debts affect your financial future.

Are You a Slave to Credit Card?

Most people are prone to the temptations of easy credit offered by credit card issuers. Nothing wrong if you pay credit card balances in full every month. But if you aren't doing so, the exorbitant interest rates will return to bite you. The banks and credit card companies are very happy to rollover your balances each month. And they really want you to slowly pay off your debts—the longer the better. Why? Because it's good business for them when you pay high interests.

To determine if you are a slave to your credit cards, ask yourself the following questions:

- Are your consumer debts making up more than 10% of your income?

- Are you having difficulty setting aside 20% of your income for savings?
- Are you paying only the minimum amount on your credit card every month?
- Are you finding it hard to pay your credit card bill in full every month?

If there is a "yes" to any of these questions, it could be a sign that your debt is overwhelming. Banks and credit card companies make big money from your debt. Your debt is their asset, but the same debt remains your liability. These companies put the power of compounding to work for them, maximizing wealth for themselves instead of you. Hence, if you still have outstanding credit card balances, make sure you settle them as soon as you possibly can. Never allow such debts to rob you of your financial future.

Moderation Is Key to Financial Success

While there is certainly an argument to be made that no debt is good debt, the fact remains that few people can afford to pay cash for everything they buy. Where debt is concerned, following the principle of "everything in moderation" is a better approach.

Remember, even debts that are determined to be good could have potentially bad downsides. Good debt can be financially destructive if you have too much of it. Just ask those people who have borrowed money for investments that made losses, or those who are still paying for their student loans long after graduation. Always remember that using debt to finance investments carry risks so it is important that you know your own risk appetite.

In my case, I don't keep any bad debt. Even with good debt, I keep it at a low level because I want to be able to sleep peacefully every night. I also want to avoid worrying about the market ups and downs. My total debt level is maintained at a level not exceeding 20% of my net worth (not income), which means I actually have enough funds to pay off all my debts at any point in time. The only reason why I choose to keep some debts is purely for tax benefits. The level of debt to maintain is very personal so there is no right or wrong answer. You need to figure out what is comfortable for you. Investors who feel they can assume greater investment risks may choose to maintain more debts, and I respect their choices.

14

Save to Invest

If you would be wealthy, think of saving as well as getting.
—Benjamin Franklin

The popular Chinese proverb tells us: "The best time to plant a tree was 20 years ago. The second-best time is now." If you plant a tree today, it will be 20 years down the road before the tree can grow into a large tree to provide shade for everybody. Wealth accumulation works the same way too. Like planting a tree, time is needed for investments to bring sizeable returns.

When you want to buy something, you won't want to worry about where you are going to get the money. You want the money immediately available for you to make that purchase, don't you? It is therefore important to start saving money as early as you can. That way, you'll have the capital available earlier to start investing to grow your wealth. Start to save at once if you have not already done so. Better to be late than never!

Why the Need to Save?

Developing a habit of saving money is the foundation of financial success. We all need to save money so we can live the lifestyle of our choice; invest and grow our money; reach our goals; and fulfill our dreams in the future. Perhaps you want to start a business one day, send your children to universities, purchase a comfortable house, or fulfill your desire to travel and experience the world. Whatever the reason may be, you need to save.

Savings will also offer you the protection of the life you have worked hard to create in case anything unplanned or unpremeditated happens. That is why it is crucial to set aside a sum of money as an emergency fund because nothing derails your life faster than unexpected events, such as a job loss or hospitalization expenses.

How much emergency fund should you save? The answer would very much depend on your current financial circumstances. A good rule of thumb is to have enough to cover six to eight months' worth of living expenses. If for any reason you lose your job, the emergency fund you have already set aside will be available to pay for necessities while you find another job.

Make Your Savings Automatic

If you find it hard to contribute to your savings account regularly, or you don't have cash left to save after all your bills are paid, you're not alone. There are many people who find it hard to save as well. Once income is deposited into the bank account, the money would soon start exiting the account to settle an endless list of bills. This isn't an uncommon problem because millions of people everywhere face a similar episode month after month. It is a vicious cycle, and one that is difficult to break.

So how do you go about breaking this vicious cycle? The answer is simple—automate your savings! Start by setting aside a comfortable amount each month to be automatically transferred to your savings account. Doing so will help make your regular savings easy and painless. As time goes by, you'll be amazed how effortless it is to live on a little less money. With today's technology, it is easy to set up an automatic savings plan. Once the portion of income is set to be deposited into your savings account every month, you won't even need to think about savings anymore.

It is human nature to spend what you can see. When you have a certain number of dollars in your wallet, you will have the tendency to spend those dollars. That is why it helps to automate the transfer of a fixed amount each month to a separate savings account. In that way, you won't be able to spend what isn't in your wallet or spending budget.

As with most good habits, starting a saving habit isn't easy. However, you will be encouraged to save more once you see your savings grow over a period of time. Saving money will become a habit without any effort on your part once it is being put on autopilot mode. That is quite a huge load taken off you! If there is still money left after paying all your bills, save the excess money for investing later.

Can Saving Alone Make You Rich?

Can you become massively rich just by saving? Very little chance. It is extremely difficult, if not impossible, for anyone to become wealthy by saving money alone. To build wealth, we need to shift our focus from money accumulation to wealth creation. Wealth building involves accumulating as many assets as possible. Your aim shouldn't be to hoard money, but to acquire assets with the purpose of increasing your overall cash flow.

In this book, I shall only classify things that generate income as assets. Simply put, anything that is making you money is an asset. Any other thing will be a liability if it doesn't generate income for you. For example, the car that you have for personal use is treated as a liability because it doesn't make you money. What's more, you need to incur petrol, maintenance, insurance and other expenses for driving the car. Hence, see your car as a liability although the accountant will classify it under "assets" in your balance sheet.

If saving money is your only strategy to building wealth, it would be difficult for you to acquire substantial wealth. How many really rich people have you come across who become wealthy just by investing in savings accounts? Can you think of anyone? No one? I rest my case then. Until now, I have yet to come across anyone who is able to build massive wealth just by saving money. The wealthy will take advantage of opportunities, solving problems, and meeting needs to propel them to achieving substantial wealth. They don't just leave their money in savings accounts.

I'm not against saving, really, and must reiterate that we all need to save money. However, it's what you are saving your money for that makes the real difference in your financial success. In fact, saving is extremely important if you want to be rich. Your savings provides the ammunition to fight the investment war in the future. You can't invest if you don't have the financial means. And you are likely to be getting your means for investing using the excess money from your savings account.

Money Will Lose Value

Money tends to lose its value in the longer term, mainly due to inflation. Every currency, be it the dollar, euro, yuan, yen, pound, franc, and you name it, will continue to depreciate in value constantly. The value of the currency and what it would buy ten years ago can't be compared to what it could buy today. Things have certainly gotten a lot more expensive these days.

Leaving your money in the bank causes money to depreciate drastically because the interest earned could hardly cover the inflation rate most of the time. The following table illustrates how money is eroded due to the effect of inflation over different periods of time.

Assuming an inflation rate of 3% per year, the estimated value of your money in today's terms would be:

Amount today	in 5 years	in 10 years	in 20 years
$1,000	$863	$744	$554
$5,000	$4,313	$3,720	$2,768
$10,000	$8,626	$7,441	$5,537
$50,000	$43,130	$37,205	$27,684
$100,000	$86,261	$74,409	$55,368

As you can see, with an inflation rate of 3%, the value of your money will almost be halved in 20 years in terms of your purchasing power. That is devastating to your financial future should you have your money idling in the bank. You are actually getting poorer as time passes because the interest rate given by the banks are much lower than the inflation rate. Your investment returns must cover at least the inflation rate to preserve the value of your money.

Money Must Be Invested to Increase Wealth

Even though savings alone won't make you rich, never stop saving a portion of your income by all means. Money must be saved first to be invested later for the purpose of building wealth. The rich understand this very well. They are constantly looking out for opportunities to invest their money, so that their money will be working hard to make even more money for them.

To be rich, your investment returns must be higher than the inflation rate. This way, the value of your assets will be higher going into the future. There are many ways to invest your money. You can invest in stocks, mutual funds, real estate investment trusts, commodities, businesses, properties, and so on. Choose one, or even a few, and become an expert in it.

The Things That Make People Rich Are Hidden

Have you played the popular Monopoly board game before? In Monopoly, the player who can accumulate the most assets will win the game. You can never win the game just by collecting the $200 salary each time you pass "GO". If all you do is collecting salary without acquiring assets, you'll end up bankrupt in no time as you pay other players for patronizing their properties.

The Monopoly game concept of building wealth is very similar to what rich people do in the real world. The wealthy invest in income-generating assets to build their wealth, while most people simply go round in circles to earn their salary every month.

Unfortunately, the majority of people choose to play their real game of life this way—collecting salaries, spending on consumables, saving the money left (if any), borrowing more to spend more on consumables, and doing every other thing except investing in assets to generate more income. No wonder so many people are broke! That also explains why the majority of people find it almost impossible to become rich, and why so many are not financially free.

Assets that the wealthy own are generally "invisible" to the public. Landlords don't carry around their property titles to show off how many properties they own. The rich don't bring along share certificates or gold bars when they go out to meet friends. Do you carry with you bank statements or certificates of deposit when you go shopping, in case you bump into friends and wish to brag how much money you have? I'm sure you don't, correct?

The things that make people rich are usually hidden from plain sight. These things are assets that would probably increase in value over time. They are things like:

- Fixed deposits or certificates of deposit
- Bonds
- Stocks
- Mutual funds
- Real estate investment trusts
- Investment properties
- Business entities

On the other hand, the things which make people gauge whether a person is rich or otherwise, are normally visible to people, and frequently proudly displayed. These things are generally liabilities that mostly don't increase in value over time. They also don't generate any income for you. Following are some examples:

- Luxury cars
- Designer clothes
- Branded accessories
- Dazzling jewelries

- Latest gadgets
- Exotic vacations
- Expensive meals

None of these liabilities actually makes you money. And not only do they not make you money, most of these things (like cars, clothes and gadgets) lose value over time, or even instantly (like an expensive meal). For example, a car loses value immediately after you bought it. You will be losing thousands of dollars if you decide to sell the car just after one day! Liabilities, unlike assets, will continue to depreciate and lose more value when they grow older.

There are always exceptions of course. For example, certain luxury watches may increase in value years later when the prices of new watches gradually increase. There are also individuals buying rare or limited-edition handbags for reselling online for profits. However, such online selling activities are best classified as businesses as the products aren't for personal enjoyment, but used to generate profits. In such a scenario, the branded handbag would be asset to the seller (who makes a profit by selling the handbag) and a liability to the buyer (who buys the handbag for personal use).

If you want to be rich, buy assets first because they bring you profits, and buy liabilities last because they cost you losses. Make an effort to acquire the assets that are mostly hidden from public. That's because these things will not only make you rich, but keep you rich as well!

15

The Power of Compounding

*Compound interest is the eighth wonder of the world.
He who understands it, earns it ... he who doesn't ... pays it.*
—Albert Einstein

Investing is all about making money grow over time. And time is critical because of the power of compounding. Compounding has a snowballing effect on your earnings, so your money would grow faster and faster as the years rolled by. With compound interest, you will gain returns not only on the money originally invested, but also on the interest it earns. Therefore, it is best to give your money as much time as possible to maximize your returns.

Start Investing Early

John and Mary are childhood friends of the same age. Both of them plan to retire at 65 and wanted to have a sum of money for their retirement. So, they invested their money yielding 10% returns per year.

John started investing an annual sum of $1,000 at 18 years old for ten years till the age of 27. And John intends to stay invested until he reaches 65 years old before taking out the funds for his retirement.

Mary, on the other hand, invested her money later at the age of 28, ten years after John started investing and after he made the final $1,000 contribution. She contributed $1,000 annually for 38 years till the age of 65 so she could have the funds for her retirement.

By the time John and Mary reach 65 years old, who do you think will have more money?

Now, the total amount of money invested by John and Mary are $10,000 ($1,000 x 10) and $38,000 ($1,000 x 38) respectively. However, John will eventually get a profit of $683,000 at 65 (excluding his $10,000 capital invested), while Mary will only get about $362,000 of profit (excluding her $38,000 contribution) at the same age. Despite the fact that Mary invested $28,000 more, John will get a whopping $321,000 additional profit because he invested earlier, and remained invested without withdrawing his money. Although Mary's investment capital is almost four times more than John, she earns about two times less than him.

You stand to gain much more if you invest a smaller sum of money now and stay invested for a longer period of time, than waiting until you have a larger amount of money to invest later. It therefore pays to start investing as early as possible, and to stay invested for as long as possible, in order to reap the best possible profit.

Let's take a look at another example to illustrate the benefit of staying invested for a longer period of time. Say you invest $10,000 at 12% returns compounding annually. At the end of ten years, you will have about $31,000. At the end of 20 years, you shall be getting $96,500. If you stay invested and take out the money at the end of 30 years, you will gain close to $300,000! That is almost ten times more profit should you decide to let your money continue to grow after ten years without cashing out your investment. If you can, always remain invested so you can maximize your nest egg for retirement.

Compounding Amplifies Wealth Accumulation

It is reasonable for investors to achieve a return on investment (ROI)—which measures the gain (or loss) generated on an investment relative to the amount invested—of around 8% to 12%. Take for example, the Vanguard 500 Index Fund Investor Shares (VFINX), issued by Vanguard on August 31, 1976, has generated an average annual return of 11.01% as of 2017 since its inception.

The following table shows the profit of an investment of just $1,000 a year at different return on investment (ROI) and various time frame:

Profit for investment of $1,000 per year (excluding total contributions by investor)					
ROI	in 5 years	in 10 years	in 20 years	in 30 years	in 40 years
5%	$802	$3,207	$14,719	$39,761	$86,840
8%	$1,336	$5,645	$29,423	$92,346	$239,781
10%	$1,716	$7,531	$43,003	$150,943	$446,852
12%	$2,115	$9,655	$60,699	$240,293	$819,142
15%	$2,754	$13,349	$97,810	$469,957	$2,005,954
20%	$3,930	$21,150	$204,026	$1,388,258	$8,772,629

From the illustration above, we can see that it pays to invest early and stay invested longer for compound interest to work to your advantage. A savvy investor making an investment of $1,000 per year at 15% rate of return would have earned a profit of more than $2 million in 40 years, with an investment capital of just $40,000. If the same investor gets a return of 20%, that profit will grow to about $8.8 million! Can you imagine the profits that could be generated by those who invested more than $1,000 every year?

The S&P 500 has delivered annualized returns averaging 9.7%, including dividends, since 1965. Warren Buffett's company, Berkshire Hathaway, has generated an average stock price gain of 20.8% per year, more than double that of the S&P 500. It's no wonder that the power of compounding has helped Buffett to stay as one of the world's richest people today.

THE POWER OF COMPOUNDING

Compounding can amplify and accelerate the growth of your investments. Time and reinvesting make compounding work better. Keep your hands off both the principal and earned profits to allow compounding to work its best if you want to gain massive returns.

Compounding Can Make You a Millionaire

The power of compounding can create millionaires from average people. According to the Bureau of Labor Statistics (BLS), the median wage for workers in the United States in the fourth quarter of 2017 was $857 per week or $44,564 per year.

Taking the annual income of $45,000, if you save and invest 10% of your income or $4,500 per year starting at the age of 30, and assuming an investment return of 10%, you'll be having a total of about $1.35 million when you reach 65 years old as shown in the chart below. Can you imagine if you start five years earlier at 25 years old? The total amount of money you will be getting at 65 would then be a staggering $2.2 million!

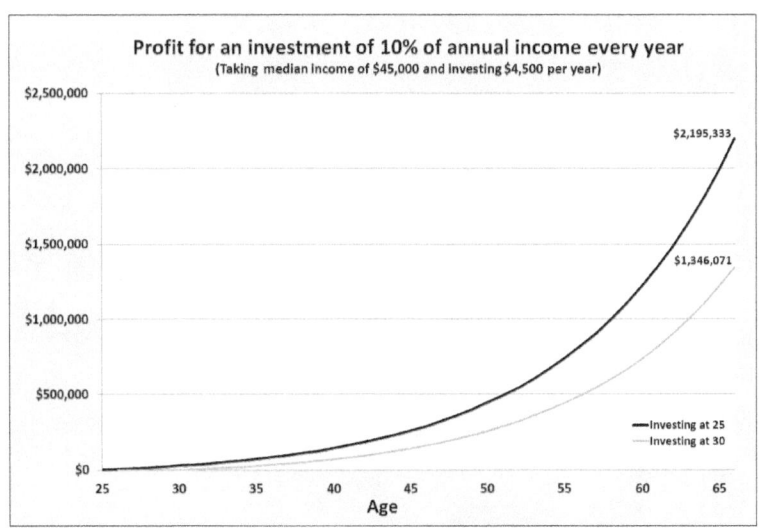

This is just a conservative projection of 10% returns. What if you are earning higher returns? In all probability, you could be earning 12% or more returns should you get your investments right most of the time. Your salary could also be increasing over time and henceforth permits you to invest more than 10% of your income. If that is the case, your end result could be much better by the time you retire. That's the power of compound interest, which is your ally to help you build wealth. The earlier you start investing and the longer you stay invested, the richer you will get. Nothing in this world can prevent your wealth from growing with compound interest on your side.

16

Take Calculated Risks

Risk comes from not knowing what you're doing.
—Warren Buffett

Life is full of risks and it is unavoidable. We all face risks every day of our lives. Everything that we do has an element of risk since no outcome can be 100% certain. Hence, any attempt at anything has a chance of complete failure. The kind of life we will end up living would very much depend on the risks we take, and the choices we make.

It is human nature to avoid risks. Millions of people around the world prefer to play it safe in most aspects of their lives. People desire success, but are afraid of failure at the same time. Yet, it is also a fact that success involves risk-taking and requires risking failure. The common success advice—go to school, study hard, get a good degree, then find a good job—becomes a mantra that most of us has been accustomed to for decades. It helps explain why the majority of people decide not to take risks to venture elsewhere other than their traditional jobs.

Not taking any forms of risk is equivalent to having a pessimistic outlook on success. Excuses for not taking risks to explore new opportunities include:

- I'm getting old already.
- I don't have much experience.
- No point looking for another job.
- I don't know how to start a business.
- Most people fail in business.
- I have no time to build a business.
- What will my family and friends think?
- I can't afford to fail.

Ask any wealthy individuals how they got so successful, and they will likely tell you that they take risks to venture out of their comfort zones. People remain average because they dislike change and prefer to play it safe. The fear of the unknown prevents many from taking on new opportunities that could bring them to a new level of success. Poor people would say, "What if I start a business and it goes belly up down the road?" Sure, there are indeed statistics indicating that nine out of ten businesses will fail. The odds are stacked against someone starting a business because there is a 90% likelihood the business would go under.

How do the wealthy think? And what will they do? Instead of focusing on the 90% chance that a business startup could fail, rich people would simply focus on the 10% chance that a business will succeed. Successful people, along with their rich mindset, might just move on to start ten business entities in order to secure a 100% chance of success! Fortune sides with those who do and dare most of the time.

In reality, many wealthy people failed many times before they finally succeed and got where they are today. Many billionaires and millionaires failed in at least three business ventures. Some of them bounced back after being broke or bankrupt. And most of them are still wealthy today.

On the other hand, people who are average or poor have never lost a business—that is because they never get themselves into setting up businesses in the first place. They probably also have not experienced bankruptcy before. Yet, many of them are struggling to pay bills, and are living paycheck to paycheck.

TAKE CALCULATED RISKS

What makes the difference? The rich take calculated risks whereas the poor don't. Never be too risk averse until you don't do anything at all. Because doing so won't lead you anywhere near to becoming wealthy.

Taking Risk Leads to Success

People don't take risks because they are afraid of failing. The wealthy understand that if they don't take some calculated risks, they have already failed. Think about it, will a growing baby eventually start walking without taking the first step and risk falling down? Failing won't make you a failure. Not trying will. Successful people aren't those who have never failed. They fail, learn from past mistakes, try again and again until they eventually succeed.

Think about the last time you learn how to cycle. You paddle to move the bicycle, learn how to balance, risk falling to the ground when you go off-balance, try again until you can finally cycle with confidence. You surely can't steer a stationary bicycle. Yes, you won't fall if you just remain seated on the bicycle and don't paddle, but you will also stay in the same spot without going anywhere!

Wealth creation certainly requires you to take some risks too. Where financial success is concerned, avoiding risks at all cost is actually riskier, and could even be costlier. You must be willing to invest in yourself by reading more books and articles to develop your financial knowledge; and following that, with your acquired knowledge, take calculated risks and proceed to invest. It might be starting your own business; investing in bonds, stocks or mutual funds; buying properties for rental income; or whatever new opportunities you plan to undertake. According to some studies, more than half of the world's self-made millionaires invested their savings in a startup or other private businesses, while the rest invested in various investment vehicles such as stocks, mutual funds, commodities and real estates.

The general rule of thumb is that the higher the risk, the higher the potential return. Understanding the relationship between risk and reward is key in forming your personal investment guideline. You also must determine your risk tolerance, and where your comfort level is, to properly assess the types of investment suitable for you. The amount of investment risk undertaken is a very personal decision for any individual investor. There is no right or wrong level of risk. If you are a young investor, you can afford to take higher risk than older investors as you have more time to recover in case you make losses in your investments. However, if you are already 65 years old and retired, you may not want to assume high investment risks. This is because you will have lesser time left to recover should you encounter significant losses from your investments.

The most common type of investment risk involves the danger of you losing money in instances where your capital isn't protected. Of course, you can still put your money in safer investments such as fixed deposits, or even bonds, but the profits you make out of them will be little as compared to other investments that provide the opportunity for better returns. For example, U.S. Treasury bonds and bills carry the full faith and credit of the United States behind them, which makes these investments one of the safest in the world. Certificates of deposit (CDs) with a federally insured bank are also very secure.

However, for the price of this security, you shall be getting a much lower return on your investment when compared to other investments such as stocks or real estates. Furthermore, when you consider the effects of inflation on your investment together with the taxes you need to pay on the gains from your profits, your investments may yield very little in real growth. Investments which are safe and comfortable will rarely earn you high profits.

Invest, Don't Gamble

Gambling is entertaining and exciting, but it produces no value to society apart from entertainment. The motivation for gambling is often to get rich instantly, without having to put in the effort to think and work hard. Many people believe gambling can make them rich, or so they imagine. However, little do they know that the odds are actually stacked against them. That is why casinos—a $261 billion industry in the U.S. according to the American Gaming Association—are highly profitable businesses.

Investing, on the other hand, is entirely different. It isn't fun, and it won't bring you the same excitement and thrill like gambling does. Investing is more like watching trees grow because it's supposed to take a long period of time. It might even take 20 to 40 years of your time for your investments to bring you substantial wealth. Any successful investor, unlike a speculator or trader, will tell you that good investment returns aren't made by buying and selling in the short-term. Rather, investments must be viewed long-term, and given enough time for them to return some serious profits for the investors.

Without a doubt, all investments involve calculated risks, unlike gambling risk which depend purely on luck. If done correctly and diligently, investing will make you rich. But the same can't be said for gambling. Investing will only be like gambling if you put money into business ventures, stocks, mutual funds, properties, or any other investments without truly knowing what you are doing. Never invest in anything that you don't understand completely, even if you are finding a lot of people making money out of it.

Is Winning the Lottery the Fastest Way to Wealth?

Some people think the easiest and quickest path to riches is by winning the lottery. Another way of looking at lottery is that it is a tax on people who can't calculate. If you are to scrutinize the probability of you winning the lottery, I believe you won't even waste a dollar on it. Unless you fail all mathematics tests in school, I think you should give lottery a miss because the chance of you striking it rich with lottery is next to none. Really, isn't this equivalent to just buying hope?

Yet, even with the odds of winning the lottery nearing impossible, a third of Americans believe that lottery offers them the best chance of becoming rich effortlessly. According to the Massachusetts state lottery, the odds of winning in Powerball is one in 175,223,510, or roughly 175 million to one! If you still believe in the odds of winning the lottery, you shouldn't be flying on a plane anymore because the odds of people being killed in a plane crash are 25 million to one. You also shouldn't be driving because the chances of people dying in a car accident are 5,000 to one. An interesting research conducted in the U.S. has determined that a person driving ten miles to buy a lottery ticket is three times more likely to die in a car accident than winning the lottery. Therefore, people are more likely to die in accidents involving a car or a plane than to win the lottery! What's more, studies have also shown that winning the lottery does not necessarily make you happier or healthier.

Most Lottery Winners Go Broke

Do you know that the majority of the lucky multimillion-dollars lottery winners are more likely to declare bankruptcy within three to five years than the average American? According to the National Endowment for Financial Education, 70% of the people who have won lotteries actually end up broke in just a few years. How is it possible that people can still go broke even with the millions of dollars they have won? That's unbelievable, isn't it?

You see, when ordinary people suddenly become very rich, they could lose all sense of reality. These newly minted multimillionaires think they have a bottomless pit of money and that they are all powerful now. They innocently believe that their riches are able to sustain whatever they do. They give away large amount of cash to family and friends. And they squander their money on luxury cars, holiday bungalows, exotic vacations, 10 carat diamonds, and whatever luxuries you can think of. With the massive windfall, lottery winners often invest in businesses they have no clue about, and without understanding the real risks involved. Even with their obscene wealth, it's easy to lose it all if they don't track their money movement and continue their careless spending. That's why most lottery winners go broke within a few years. No wonder people in the finance industry joke that if you really want to get back at your enemies, give them a lottery ticket!

Don't gamble away your hard-earned money because the chances of people making a fortune by gambling are simply too slim. Learn to be more investment-savvy instead. Investing your money wisely to build wealth is the best path to riches, not trying your luck at gambling.

17

Develop Other Income Streams

*If you don't find a way to make money while you sleep,
you will work until you die.*
—Warren Buffett

The last two decades should have taught us at least one lesson: that no job is safe. The official unemployment rate provided by the authorities often conceals troubling realities—a growing number of graduates overqualified for their existing jobs, a vast number of contract workers with no real job security, and legions of part-time workers desperate for full-time jobs. The day is fast-approaching where humans will lose most of the jobs to robots, automation and technology. A reliable nine-to-five job is quickly disappearing beyond anyone's control. Unfortunately for most people, their only source of income is from their full-time job. Many would find themselves struggling financially should they lose their jobs.

Some would argue that their deposits in the banks are paying them monthly interest income. However, with the low interest rates for savings account, the interest earned is far too little to be considered as another source of income. To put it in proper perspective, even if you have $100,000 in your savings account, taking the national average of 0.08% annual interest rate in the United States, it would only earn you interest of $800 annually or a measly $66.67 per month. Moreover, how many people have a six-digit amount in their savings accounts?

Data from Magnify Money tells us that the average American household's savings account balance is $16,420, while the median savings account balance across American households is $4,830. Notice that the median savings account balance is considerably lower than the average savings? This means that most people have much lesser savings than the average amount of $16,420, which also means that most households would be having only a four-digit amount in their savings accounts.

Even with $10,000 in the savings account, the interest income with an interest rate of 0.08% is just $6.67 each month—barely helpful to anyone. Will adding the interest income to your monthly salary make a significant difference to your finances? It certainly won't. For most people, just one main source of income from their paychecks aren't good enough to help them get substantially richer. In today's uncertain world, with its accompanying economic instability, the better solution for financial security is to develop multiple income streams instead of just depending on one source of paycheck income. Wealthy people, on the other hand, almost certainly have other sources of income besides their salaries.

If you wish to secure your financial future, it is better that you start planning to develop other income streams over and above what you are already earning now. The best time to repair the roof is on a sunny day, not when it is raining. Hence, people will be better off building up other income streams when they are still having their day jobs, not when they become jobless. Developing your income sources is crucial for your financial success. Do it sooner rather than later because you will need time to develop as well as to stabilize alternate income streams.

Difference Between Active and Passive Income

During the process of wealth building, your money needs to be working for you round-the-clock even when you are asleep. For that to happen, you would need passive income. Before you begin exploring ideas to diversify your income streams, first understand the difference between the two broad categories of income—active income and passive income.

I choose to classify portfolio income (income derived from dividends, interest and capital gains) under passive income instead. This is because they are income earned indirectly. Others prefer to put portfolio income as a third category of income over and above active and passive income. Please don't get too worried over such classification of income as it isn't really that crucial. What's important is that you know the differentiation between what's active income and what's not.

1. Active Income

Most of us should be familiar with active income. It is income paid to people when they work in traditional jobs. This includes salaries, wages, commissions, tips and any other income from businesses that requires your time and effort. With active income, your active participation is involved. Once you stop doing the work, your income stops immediately. You can't be hands-off earning active income.

2. Passive Income

Passive income, on the other hand, is income paid to you without your active participation in the work. It is money earned indirectly where you're totally hands-off, most of the time at least. This is where income is earned when you put your money to work for you, instead of you working for the money.

Some common types of passive income include interest from savings and fixed deposit accounts, dividends from stocks, rental income from properties, annuities, royalties, and any other businesses that earn you income without requiring your active involvement.

Why Is Passive Income Important?

I'm assuming you want to be wealthy and you wish to know how. Let me give you a hint: You probably will never get wealthy working for your boss. Why? Because business owners or entrepreneurs buy your time and expertise to make themselves rich, not you.

Very few employees in this world will get massively rich. The Credit Suisse 2018 report stated that there are 42 million millionaires around the world. Now, this figure seems like there are lots of millionaires everywhere, doesn't it? However, out of the 7.7 billion people living in the world today, only 0.5% are really rich. It also means that 99.5% of the world population are not millionaires. The same report tells us that anyone having a net worth of around $800,000 will put that person at the top 5% of people in the whole world. The report also stated that among the wealthy people, most are business owners; very few are employees. So, what do these statistics tell us? It confirms that the vast majority of employees are not that rich. A separate survey also found that almost 80% of American workers live from one paycheck to another.

Some would argue that there are top management executives earning salaries in the millions. But these executives are few and far between. How many chief executive officers are there in companies or organizations? Yes, there's only one CEO in most organizations. There are also very few senior executives sitting at top management levels in any corporation. The majority of workers are lower management employees, with some at middle management level.

Sure, there will also be some who have jobs that pay a six-figure salary per annum. These people are rich solely with their active income and need not have to worry about paying bills. But then again, they don't represent the majority.

Most people are actually earning a five-figure income annually. This is confirmed by the data collected by the United States Census Bureau's American Community Survey. The following table shows the median total income for full-time, year-round employees by age:

Median Total Income by Age					
Age	Median Income	Age	Median Income	Age	Median Income
20	$20,600	37	$50,000	54	$55,000
21	$22,000	38	$50,000	55	$54,500
22	$24,000	39	$51,000	56	$55,000
23	$26,100	40	$50,000	57	$54,300
24	$30,000	41	$52,000	58	$55,000
25	$34,000	42	$52,000	59	$55,000
26	$35,000	43	$52,400	60	$54,000
27	$37,000	44	$53,000	61	$55,000
28	$40,000	45	$53,000	62	$55,200
29	$40,000	46	$55,000	63	$56,000
30	$42,000	47	$55,000	64	$58,000
31	$44,000	48	$55,000	65	$59,700
32	$45,000	49	$55,000	66	$62,000
33	$45,000	50	$54,000	67	$66,000
34	$47,000	51	$55,000	68	$67,500
35	$49,500	52	$55,000	69	$68,000
36	$50,000	53	$54,000	70	$72,000

Source: Business Insider calculations with 2017 American Community Survey IPUMS. Table shows median total income for full-time, year-round workers.

The salaries of full-time employees tend to vary by age, with older workers earning more than younger workers as can be seen in the median income table. The following shows the line chart of the median total personal income for workers at each year of age:

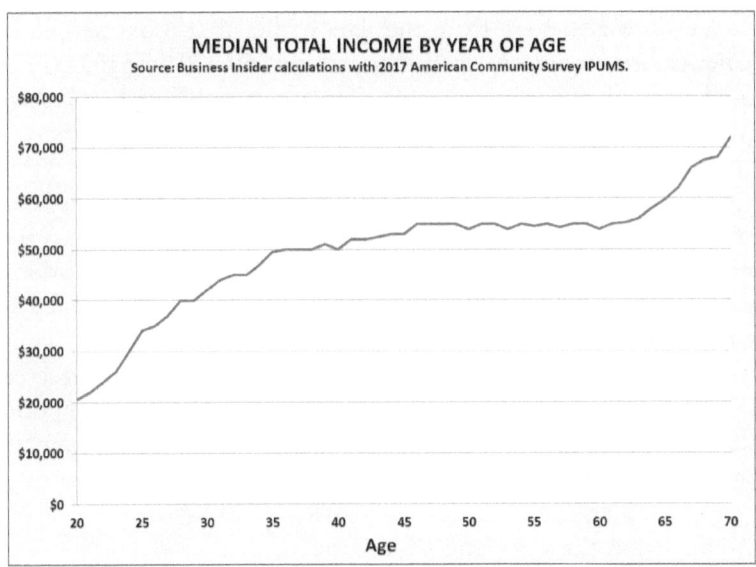

From the line chart above, we can see an interesting pattern. The income earned by full-time employees tend to increase with age among workers in their 20s to mid-30s. However, there is a plateau in income among workers from their late 30s to early 60s where the median income is about $50,000 to $55,000. The median income will only continue to trend upwards should the employees continue full-time work past the normal retirement age of 65.

Make Your Money Work for You

We have already discovered in the earlier chapter the reasons why most people aren't rich. Coincidentally, they are also the ones with only one stream of income—the salaries from their jobs. Wealthy people, on the other hand, never rely on their salaries alone to build their wealth. They have passive income streams as well. And the majority of wealthy people have passive income streams from various investments that hugely exceed their salaries (or active income).

We have also seen from the data earlier that most people in America are earning median incomes of $50,000 to $55,000 for most part of their working life. Most can only hope for their salaries to increase if they choose to work beyond 65 years old, which means that they will have to retire much later. I believe this is far from what most people would desire. To be rich, you need to ensure that your money is working hard for you and not the other way round. But the sad fact is that most people are working hard for the money. For the wealthy, however, the money is working hard for them and making them money even while they're asleep. According to author Tom Corley, who conducted a five-year study of the daily habits of both the rich and the poor, most self-made millionaires generated their income from not one, but a few other income sources:

- 65% has three streams of income
- 45% has four streams of income
- 29% has five or more streams of income

From Corley's study, we can conclude that the majority of self-made millionaires have at least three sources of income. These additional income streams include rentals from investment properties, profits from side hustle businesses, and stock market investments.

To gain substantial wealth, you need to expand your means beyond just one income stream. Having multiple income streams give you more financial security. During an economic downturn of which you have no control over, when one stream of income is negatively affected (for example property rental), your other income streams (such as stock dividends) can cover up the losses. Hence, your overall income streams will allow you to survive the downturn without seeing your lifestyle dramatically affected. Let's assume you are a McDonald's franchise owner with ten fast-food stores at different locations. Say three of your stores aren't bringing you profits while the other seven outlets are still providing you with healthy cash flows. In this case, your overall profits would still be healthy because the seven profitable outlets are able to cover the shortfalls of those three unprofitable ones.

Try to find ways to make additional passive income. Investing in equities, mutual funds, or REITs (real estate investment trusts) that give regular dividends will add to your income sources. Purchasing another property for rental income is another good source of passive income.

If you own an investment property, try to have your property tenanted all the time so you can enjoy ongoing rental income. When experiencing housing market downturns, ensure that you minimize vacancy even if it means lowering rent to attract tenants to your property. It's better to have at least some rent coming in than none at all, especially when you still have a mortgage loan to pay. Never invest in any property just for potential capital appreciation and missed out rental income in the meantime.

It's worth repeating—never leave your idle money in the bank because the interest income is simply too little, and you won't be able to beat inflation most of the time. Always remain focus on generating additional income by investing in things that bring you passive income streams. This is what the wealthy do to get to where they are.

Start with Active Income, Build up Passive Income

Active income is where everybody gets started—with their first job, startup, business venture, or whatever things they do to make money with their active participation. To be substantially rich, however, you need more than just active income. It is interesting to note that most millionaires have at least three different sources of passive income.

Most people need to start building up passive income in order to create lifelong financial security. If money isn't made while you are sleeping, you are likely to be working till you die. Hence, it is hard to be wealthy if your salary is the only source of income. As you start off with active income, you have to manage your money well and continue to think of ways to build up passive income. Over time, the amount of passive income you earned could well be overtaking your active income. This is the best way to secure your financial future. In addition, having substantial passive income allows you to recalibrate your life to gradually scale back your active income efforts. You may, for instance, want to switch your current stressful job to one that works fewer hours so you can have more quality time with your family.

Passive income can be the key to a happier and fruitful life. It is also the difference between living comfortably and living well. You become financially free when your passive income exceeds your living expenses. Financial independence allows you to have an additional option to quit your nine-to-five job and escape the rat race. While other workers are forced to stay employed, you have earned more options with your passive income. You now work because you *want* to, not because you *need* to. That's a world of difference. Because you are always ready to retire anytime you decide to live your dream life without any worry about the loss of your salary.

Passive Income Doesn't Mean Zero Work

The idea behind passive income is that you earn regular income from a system you have built without having to do any additional work to maintain it. What's not to love about earning money from this system in your sleep?

However, don't misunderstand and think that all passive income involves no work. In some passive income instances, work and constant attention are still required, especially during the initial stages. It's just that your income isn't directly tied to the number of hours that you put into the work, unlike full-time employees earning their salaries or wages.

For example, before you can earn rental income from a property, much work is involved both before and after the purchase of the investment property. You need to research the property market; attend numerous viewings; negotiate with owners and agents; manage property agents; speak with lawyers and tax accountants; and file your taxes on a regular basis.

If you are starting a blog or website with the aim of making money through affiliate marketing, selling products online, or earning some advertising income, many hours of work are also involved. Bloggers need to put in lots of hard work to constantly write useful content for their target audiences. Hence, there are ongoing work and marketing efforts involved.

Similarly, before anyone can earn royalty income from publishing a book, much time and efforts have to be put in to complete the entire book project. Take this book as an example. It took me many months (years even) of extensive research; reading newspapers, books, magazines and articles; and countless late nights writing the manuscript. And after more than 58,000 written words later, this book became a reality! For any book to achieve reasonable success after it has been launched, the author will need to interact with readers, network with other authors, maintain a growing email list, keep up with social media, respond to reviews, and so on. Which also means there is an enormous amount of work that the author needs to put in on a continual basis.

Other examples of truly passive income are interest income from savings accounts or certificate of deposits, and dividends from stocks or REITs (real estate investment trusts). That is where you invest money upfront and keep earning the income generated automatically. In these cases, you might not need to do much other than some active maintenance work once in a while, like rebalancing your investment portfolio periodically.

The idea of passive income is undeniably awesome, but it is a lot more subjective and complex in practice than it is in theory. The examples mentioned are all great options for earning passive income and securing your financial future. You just need to get yourself ready for some upfront work, and probably some ongoing work as well.

PART THREE

STAY RICH

If we command our wealth, we shall be rich and free.
If our wealth commands us, we are poor indeed.
—Edmund Burke

Getting rich is not the most difficult part of the financial success journey. Staying rich is. It is hard for the wealthy to remain rich because it involves discipline and commitment. Good wealth accumulation and preservation strategies are also needed. In order to stay rich, wealthy individuals must continue to live below their means. They must also stay invested for their money to continue growing, and manage their investments prudently under changing economic conditions.

While it is true that not everyone can get rich, for those who do become rich, staying rich can become a greater challenge. This is because the more riches they accumulate, the greater the temptation for them to live lavishly. With more money, people would have the means to live a more luxurious lifestyle. It becomes easier for them to buy bigger houses, drive better cars, go for more exotic vacations, wear more designer labels, eat more expensive meals, and the list continues. How many really rich people do you know who don't behave like they're wealthy, and live a simpler life than most ordinary people?

Having said that, there are also many wealthy people who are surprisingly frugal despite their massive wealth. That's the reason why these people are rich, and why they remain rich till this day. One of the world's richest people, Azim Premji (an Indian business tycoon who was the former executive chairman of Wipro Limited), is a good example of a billionaire who lives frugally. Even with a net worth of about $9 billion as of January 2021, Premji still flies in economy class, drives secondhand cars, and always reminds his employees to turn off the lights at the office. However, despite living a frugal life, Premji is a very generous person. According to *Forbes*, the Azim Premji Foundation pledged $134 million to provide aid for those affected by the COVID-19 pandemic in April 2020.

Rich people stay rich by living as if they are broke, whereas broke people remain broke by living like they are rich. Always remember: The key to staying rich is to make your money work harder for you, while you continue to live a simple and frugal life.

18

Live a Frugal Life

Beware of little expenses. A small leak will sink a great ship.
—Benjamin Franklin

Frugal living involves you making intentional spending choices. Granted, an occasional splurge or indulgence might not cause a dent to the rich, but frequent frivolous spending can certainly erode their net worth very quickly. In fact, there are many millionaires, and even billionaires, who choose to live frugally even though they can afford to buy almost anything in this world with their massive wealth. Wealthy people possess a level of discipline in order to become rich, and stay rich. Remember this: The biggest barrier for people to becoming rich is living like they are rich before they really are.

What Is Frugal Living?

It is a myth that living a frugal life means living a boring life. Many people are just assuming that all frugal people sit at home all day doing nothing, except staring at the walls. Others think living frugally means living cheaply. But this is far from the truth! Sadly, there are enough people who are not interested in frugal living because they believe in this myth. The truth is, frugality has nothing to do with being cheap or making cheap choices. It is merely being intentional. One must be resourceful, not wasteful, to be frugal.

To me, frugal living doesn't mean you can't enjoy material things. It means you don't stretch yourself financially just to enjoy the finer things in life. Frugal living involves good money discipline and wise management of finances. I will never recommend anyone to borrow money to buy luxury items for their own enjoyment. Frugal individuals are not misers. And they really do spend money. Just that frugal people choose to practice conscious spending, prioritizing purchases to ensure money are spent to acquire things that are truly valuable.

My wealthy friends who live frugally are truly enjoying life to the fullest. Myself included. Many of my friends think I'm living a boring life, and missing out on life simply because I choose to live frugally all these years, despite being a millionaire. Sometimes, I wonder why would they think this way, bearing in mind that I own a bungalow with a nice swimming pool for my retirement living. I bought the bungalow—an asset that appreciates in value over time—without any borrowing so I won't incur unnecessary debt during my retirement years. I'm also able to spend quality time with my family, and go on family vacations a few times a year. Sure, I do buy little luxuries once in a blue moon, but never with borrowed money. And I won't choose to enjoy the finer things in life if I can't afford them comfortably. I surely have no lack and believe I'm living the best life I possibly could, doing whatever I choose to do with the time that I have. Hence, I shall let you decide whether frugal living is considered boring or otherwise!

Since retiring from corporate employment in 2007, I have been receiving job offers and partnership arrangements that came with attractive packages from time to time. However, I rejected those opportunities because I don't wish to sell my time, and my freedom that goes along with it, for more money. Some may think I'm foolish. But think about it for a moment. I'm now using my time to manage and grow my own investments, and in doing so, I'm essentially making myself wealthier instead of working for others to make them richer! Furthermore, the recurring income generated from my various investments more than sufficiently support the lifestyle that I'm living now.

If you aspire to be wealthy, live frugally so that you can save more money for investment later. I guarantee you will be a much happier person when you are not drowning in debt. Financial success awaits those who take positive actions to manage their finances wisely.

Learning to Be Frugal

Frugality doesn't come naturally. At least not for me. I have to learn it through the years. Most of us need to educate ourselves on how to live frugally. Having said that, it really doesn't help when we are being bombarded with so many advertisements daily telling us how we should spend our money. It's entirely up to us to filter those messages so that we won't be influenced to part with our money on unnecessary things easily.

In my case, I have learned to live frugally by first discovering the things in my life that make me truly satisfied, together with the things that I value most. I find that companionship, achievements and experiences are the things that satisfy me and make me happy; and family and health are what I value most. Once I got my satisfactions and values aligned to my purpose, my spending becomes more controlled. I'm now less tempted to buy stuffs that are out of alignment to my satisfactions and values, which in turn increase my tendency to live frugally as times passes.

Therefore, learning to be frugal is a process that you need to make a conscious effort to go through. While you're working at it, you'll get better at making spending choices over time.

How Should You Live?

Ironically, living a rich life will make you poorer, especially so when you can't afford the rich lifestyle. To live within your means, you'll have to ensure that your expenditure doesn't exceed your income. Is this still possible today with increasing prices and income remaining stagnant most of the time? Well, you still could, but it takes discipline and good money habits on your part. It would also mean that you must avoid keeping up with the Joneses and acquiring things that steal your solvency.

This then, is how you should live if you want to be wealthy…

If you plan to bring your family to Paris for a holiday, bring them to Penang instead. Choose a Rado watch when you have the money for a Rolex. Carry a Longchamp handbag when you can afford a Louis Vuitton. Wear Gap clothing when you can easily buy Gucci. See what I'm trying to drive at? Yes, drive a BMW only if you have money to buy a Bentley. You need to live well below your means. This is extremely important if you want to achieve financial success and retire financially free when the time comes.

Again, I'm not speaking against anyone enjoying some luxuries in life, especially if it is within your means to do so. Life shouldn't be all work and no play. Ideally, life should be fun and meaningful. You surely need some time off regularly to rejuvenate yourself, treat yourself to a wonderful meal, buy yourself that expensive gift you have been eyeing for some time, or go on an extended holiday with your family. Indulge in some luxuries if it is well within your means. But never borrow to finance those luxuries. Busting your budget just to own luxurious stuffs is never worth it as doing so can destroy your financial future.

Live like a "secret" rich person and you will become one. You would have succeeded in living that way if the people around you couldn't even tell that you are wealthy. Most millionaires don't live in sprawling mansions. They live well below their means. Hence, don't rush into buying your dream car or other big-ticket items on a tight budget. Buy only when you can well afford to. Learn to live below your means. Because *being* rich is far better than *looking* rich!

Frugal Habits of the Wealthy

Becoming wealthy, and staying that way, requires self-control. The frugal habits necessary to achieve financial success can be simple, but it takes a lot of discipline for the wealthy to maintain their fortunes. Wealthy people frequently make spending choices with longer term views. They choose to forgo instant gratification and focus their spending on things that can create value. It may surprise you, but there is a small subset of super-rich individuals who are well-known for their frugal lifestyles and penny-pinching ways. Allow me to draw your attention to five ultra-successful billionaires and millionaires, where we can surely take a page from their fiscally-responsible habits.

1. Warren Buffett

Legendary investor Warren Buffett, with an estimated net worth of about $88.6 billion as of January 2021, has been living in the same five-bedroom house he bought in Omaha for merely $31,500 since 1958. Although Buffett could afford the biggest mansion on earth, the multibillionaire prefers the simple life in small-town America.

Buffett revealed in a 2013 interview with *CNN* that he still used a Nokia flip phone, long after smartphones existed. "This is the one Alexander Graham Bell gave me," he joked about his phone. "I don't throw anything away until I've had it 20 or 25 years."

Buffett has been using the same black wallet for 20 years. He also shuns high-end designer suits and instead, wears suits created by a Chinese sewing entrepreneur named Madam Li.

CNBC reported that when it comes to food, the billionaire investor has been known to save money by taking the fast-food route. In fact, he might kick off his day with a trip to McDonald's during his five-minute drive to work. If he is feeling rich, he will splurge by spending $3.17 on a bacon, egg and cheese biscuit sandwich. If the market happens to be down, he might spend just $2.95 on a sausage, egg and cheese sandwich instead. On a really bad day, he buys two sausage patties for $2.61.

2. Ingvar Kamprad

The late Ingvar Kamprad, founder of IKEA, was known for his frugal habits despite his massive wealth. Upon his death at the age of 91, Kamprad was the world's eighth richest person and was worth $58.7 billion as of January 2018 according to *Bloomberg*.

The self-made billionaire always flew economy and stayed at budget hotels while traveling; cut his hair in developing countries; and even buy clothes from flea markets. *The Telegraph* reported that he said on television, "If you look at me now, I don't think I'm wearing anything that wasn't bought at a flea market."

For 20 years, Kamprad drove a 1993 Volvo 240 GL, which was only sold when someone persuaded him that driving such an old car was too dangerous. Originally, the car was worth around $22,000, but at the time he sold it, it would have been worth just a few thousand dollars.

In 1976, he penned and distributed *The Testament of a Furniture Dealer*—a pamphlet of guidelines that IKEA employees still follow to this day. Kamprad detailed pieces of his frugal philosophy in the pamphlet, stating that wasting resources is a mortal sin at IKEA.

3. David Cheriton

David Cheriton, with an estimated net worth of $8.4 billion as of January 2021, is a Stanford University professor who founded and invested in technology companies, including Google, where he was an early private investor. He has a habit of saving half of his meal for the next day when dining at restaurants. Cheriton has also been cutting his own hair for more than 20 years. Many of his frugal habits come from his parents, who grew up during the Great Depression, a severe worldwide economic depression that took place mostly during the 1930s.

The Stanford computer science professor hates the idea of living like a billionaire. "I'm actually quite offended by that sort of thing," he told the *Edmonton Journal* in a 2006 interview. "These people who build houses with 13 bathrooms and so on, there's something wrong with them." Cheriton calls himself "spoiled" for taking the occasional windsurfing vacation to Maui. When pressed by a *Forbes* interviewer to recall his latest splurge, Cheriton said that his biggest splurge was his 2012 Honda Odyssey.

4. Mitt Romney

Mitt Romney, with an estimated net worth of $280 million as of January 2021, is a businessman and the U.S. Senator from Utah. The former Republican Party presidential candidate has budget-conscious spending habits—several of which were revealed in a *New York Times* article in 2011 including using JetBlue to snag cheap airfare, tackling home renovations himself, and buying his golf clubs at Kmart.

A family friend was quoted in the same article saying that one of Romney's mottos is, "Just because you can afford something doesn't mean you should buy it."

5. Michelle Obama

Michelle Obama, the wife of Barack Obama (the 44th president of the United States), is a writer, advocacy icon, and lawyer. The former first lady launched her memoir *Becoming* on November 13, 2018. The book deal reportedly netted her over $65 million. According to *The Hollywood Reporter*, the book, *Becoming*, smashed sales expectations for both for political memoirs and nonfiction books, and had sold more than two million copies in its first 15 days across all platforms in just the United States and Canada.

Though Mrs. Obama has a net worth of $75 million (excluding what she shares with her husband) as of January 2021, she is known for being thrifty. She frequently shops at Target stores to save on everyday household items. Mrs. Obama is also known to cut costs when it comes to fashion, sometimes choosing to wear clothing from discount stores. In 2011, she appeared on the *Today* show wearing a $35 dress from H&M.

Distinguish Between Wants and Needs

To put it simply: A need is something you must have, and a want is something you desire to have. In fact, all of us need just four things to live and survive. These things are:

1. A roof over our head.
2. Sufficient water and food to maintain your health.
3. Clothing to remain comfortable and appropriately dressed.
4. Basic health care and medicinal products.

Any other things that go beyond the above list—a luxurious house, designer clothes, fine wines, high-end meals, a limousine, branded watches, exotic vacations—are wants. On the surface, the difference between wants and needs is easy to understand. However, very few people have a real understanding of the difference between needs and wants. When I asked my friends about whether something they spent on is a want or a need, most responded with a blank stare, while some replied, "What's the difference?"

Many people tend to buy what they want and not what they need. Let's be very honest. People don't need an Omega watch because a Timex will do just as well in telling accurate time. But why are luxury watches still selling so well? That's because people just want them, even though they don't need them. Owning luxury products, and displaying them publicly, often becomes a statement of success for most people; or so they believe. I wonder if people flaunting luxuries know their belief systems are often misguided—all the while being influenced by the media promoting materialism, as well as being misled by those around them who are equally misguided.

On the contrary, there are many people who really need to have insurance policies because they don't have adequate funds to cover any emergencies. However, most of them don't have insurance policies and may not even have made plans to purchase any insurance. Why? Because people don't want to think about illness, disability, or death. That explains why most insurance agents will tell you that it's extremely difficult to sell insurance.

We need to distinguish between what are our wants and needs. It is easy to disguise wants as needs, especially when we desire that something so much. Sometimes, we may want to question ourselves before purchasing things, especially for big-ticket items or any other expensive items. Make it a habit to ask yourself the following questions before buying:

- Why do I want to buy this?
- Do I really need this?
- How will this item help me?
- What is the real purpose behind this purchase?
- Are there other cheaper alternatives?
- Can I buy this same item cheaper elsewhere?
- Can I wait a little longer for price to drop before buying?
- Can I live without this thing?

Don't fool yourself with answers like: "I'm happy and just want to buy it." Such an attitude is often a precursor to financial troubles ahead. Stop it at once!

Sometimes, a person's careless spending on unnecessary stuff may be a symptom of a deeper psychological issue. Some people may want to wear expensive outfits to hide their lack of self-confidence. Others may buy expensive gifts just to impress others or to gain friendship. Reckless spending habits won't solve such problems. The joy of owning new things is often short-lived. Do some reflections on your motivations for frequent indulgence should your careless spending habits are a result of an unhealthy psychological issue. Not doing so will only add stress and lead to serious financial problems down the road.

So, does that mean that we shouldn't buy the things that we want if they are not things we need? Not at all! We want to live in this world, not merely exist. We should most definitely treat ourselves to some "wants" once in a while; but only do so when we can afford to and have the cash to buy them.

What we want and what we need aren't always the same. The difference between a want and a need is actually self-control. We shouldn't indulge in our wants using money we don't have to buy them. Instead, we must exercise self-control and be willing to delay short-term gratification for long-term financial success. Never ever borrow money to indulge!

19

The Price of Ego

Financial peace isn't the acquisition of stuff. It's learning to live on less than you make, so you can give money back and have money to invest. You can't win until you do this.
—Dave Ramsey

The more wealth one accumulates, the more temptation there is to spend more. A tug of war between ego and humility begins where most people feed the former and starve the latter. Everything in society, together with the various media, make it easy for people to let egoism prevails when they become rich.

Haven't you encounter the media blasting you with advertisements to make you drool over the lifestyle of the rich and famous? Haven't you, for once, aspire to be one of them? Billions of dollars are spent in various media to tell you what house you should live in; what car you should drive; where you should go for holidays; what watch you should wear; what smartphone you should use; what food you should eat; and whatever luxuries that come to your mind. You get the point? The media encourage you to be materialistic, and businesses want you to be addicted to a lifestyle of excessive consumption. Ultimately, the objective is to make you part your money on things they want you to spend on.

Don't Pretend to Be Rich

Tommy, my property agent, called me one day and spoke casually with me about his friend, Derek, who runs a business in Singapore distributing personal care products. According to Tommy, Derek lived a lavish life—living in an expensive house in Singapore, driving a Mercedes-Benz S400, owning three country club memberships, and often spending thousands of dollars on a single occasion in high-end restaurants. He also owns another huge bungalow with a nice swimming pool in a neighboring country as his weekend holiday home.

A few months later, I met up with Tommy again when he arranged viewings for several investment properties that I have shortlisted. During our discussion over lunch, he mentioned to me that Derek's business lost huge sums of money and that he needed to sell off his assets urgently to raise funds. Derek eventually sold his holiday home (the pool bungalow his family used to stay over the weekends) to me eight days after we started negotiation. The bungalow was purchased at a price considerably lower than its bank valuation, making it a great asset to add to my property portfolio. I have since leased out the bungalow to an expatriate, providing me with good rental income. But I didn't buy his car and country club memberships because I consider these things liabilities that won't make me any money.

You can't judge a book by its cover when it comes to personal wealth. The late Dr. Thomas J. Stanley, bestselling author of *The Millionaire Next Door*, has spent many years researching the typical life of a millionaire. His study shows many misconceptions that people still have today regarding the lifestyle of the wealthy. In his other book *Stop Acting Rich*, Stanley defines a group of people he calls "aspirationals" as people who choose to act rich, but don't have the financial resources to back it up.

Derek's story is one of the many stories of aspirationals that I have come across. I find that many people are sacrificing every cent they own just to have rich appearances, and potentially pushing themselves into financial ruins. The case of Derek is a good example. I sincerely hope that one day, he will recover from his financial struggles and start over to become a wiser financial steward.

The solution to getting rich, and staying rich is simple—stop being an aspirational! All that glitters is not gold. And all that glitters is not always the millionaire's goal!

Most Wealthy People Don't Live Lavishly

Rich people are frequently stereotyped as having extravagant lifestyles, seemingly having unlimited resources to acquire luxurious items of their desire. Is this a reality or just a fallacy concerning the lifestyle of the wealthy? While wealthy individuals (like some Hollywood celebrities and sports stars) with lavish lifestyles do exist, they are an exception rather than a norm.

It is common to see many people driving exotic cars these days. Are they supposed to be impressive just because of their fanciful cars? Do fancy cars owners equate with the highly successful people? Might not be the case. More like making unwise decisions to me, especially if they belong to the squeezed middle-class trying hard to appear rich. Can the type of car people drive represent their level of success? Surely not! Think about it, millions of people worldwide are driving cars that are more glamorous than what billionaire investor Warren Buffett drives, which is a Cadillac XTS costing him just $45,295. Are we supposed to assume that these people more successful that Buffett? Clearly, the car that one drives is not a reliable indicator of one's financial success. *The Millionaire Next Door* included the survey of self-made millionaires in America that revealed the most popular make of car among the wealthy isn't a Rolls-Royce, Bentley, or a Lamborghini, but a Toyota!

As for myself, I wouldn't think twice spending money buying assets that would generate good investment returns. But I just couldn't allow myself to spend lavishly on a top-of-the-range luxury car that won't generate any income, even though I can actually afford to drive any car that's available. Rather than keeping up with the Joneses, my wife and I choose to maintain our frugal lifestyle to ensure that we will continue to stay rich.

Don't Flaunt Your Wealth

While making money and getting rich is a fun and worthwhile activity, always be very careful with your money and resist the urge to brag about your material things. Even if you are wealthy, don't flaunt your wealth.

After you have achieved greatness and substantial wealth, you will soon come to realize that not everyone would enjoy celebrating your success together with you. You may not know it, but even your closest friends or colleagues might not be happy seeing you more successful than them. Unfortunately, you are bound to come across people who are jealous of you and aren't that happy to see you living a good life. What's worse is that their jealously could even turn to hatred down the road.

There will also be people trying to get close to you for the wrong reasons if you flaunt your wealth. At times, it could make it hard for you to distinguish between genuine friends and the fair-weather ones. Worst still, some people could also make you a target for their evil plans!

When you flash your wealth to others, you will invite criticism, envy, jealously and condemnation. Whether the person you meet will tell you honestly how he or she feels about you is another story. Most people don't. On the other hand, being frugal and humble even when you are wealthy encourages admiration, respect and emulation.

Even if you happen to be a millionaire, you shouldn't be telling others how much you are worth. Why? Because if you do, the poor may resent you for having so much; while the billionaires, who are much richer than you, could despise you for not having much more! You can never please people of both sides. So, you might as well stay silent about your wealth.

The rich are always ready to invest rather than trying to impress. Many of them don't own private jets and flashy cars; they never keep white tigers as pets; or build amusement parks for their own enjoyment. Rich people understand that for every dollar they don't waste spending on unnecessary things, they will have an extra dollar to invest. And every dollar they invest will eventually return them many folds in wealth.

The price of maintaining your ego is expensive. Very often, the root cause of your spending problem is nothing but your own ego. Instead of treating the symptom by buying expensive things that you don't need, or living an extravagant lifestyle that you shouldn't, why not address the root cause? Get rid of your ego. When ego is lost, limit is lost. You free yourself and you become infinite and kind. Don't live life the way others think you should. You need to be comfortable with what you have and be happy about how you're living your own life. An enriching life shouldn't be associated with material things, or lifestyles of the rich and famous.

20

Stop Spending Money You Don't Have

Never spend your money before you have it.
—Thomas Jefferson

Imagine yourself walking through a casino in Las Vegas. You hear people shrieking with joy with the slot machines pouring out chips after they strike jackpots. You witness players smiling at the roulette and blackjack tables with tall stacks of chips in front of them after winning bets. These are common sights every time you walk through the casinos.

The winners all seem so happy. You begin to ask yourself, "If they can play and win, I believe I can too!"

Don't be fooled by the scene you witnessed. The fact is, there are much more losers than winners. And there's a high chance that those winners will eventually become losers if they continue playing. It's simply statistically impossible to win at gambling. Otherwise, casinos will not be such bustling and profitable businesses.

Looking at the way people spend their money using credit cards remind me of the gamblers at the casinos. Why do you think all the casinos let their customers play using chips instead of cash? It may have something to do with the psychology of human beings. People won't be betting as much when using cash as compared to using chips. When gamblers place their bets with chips, they won't feel that they are using real money, just like spenders using credit cards.

Credit cards by themselves aren't evil. But many just couldn't resist the temptation to excessively use plastics to spend on things they don't have the money to pay for. That's equivalent to spending money they don't have, which often lead them to potential financial troubles ahead.

Never be tempted to spend any money you have not earned. It's so easy and convenient to swipe the plastic to get whatever you want. While it is alright to use credit to buy things you have the money to pay for, buying on credit for things you can't afford would be the worst decision you can ever made. Not only will you pay a high price by spending future money now, your future financial success is also being threatened.

Credit Card Is the Costliest Credit Facility

The Center for Microeconomic Data's report on household debt and credit reveals that total household debt has reached $13.51 trillion in the third quarter of 2018, with the total credit card debt hitting over $844 billion dollars. The survey conducted by the Consumer Financial Protection Bureau (CFPB) found that less than 40% of American consumers pay their credit card balances in full.

Credit card debts are the most expensive type of loans. Many people incurred debts using credit cards just to satisfy their never-ending consumption appetite. The costs of such debts are high when banks and credit card companies charging anywhere from 16% to 24% interest per annum. Most credit card companies allow you to pay just a fraction of your expenses and you can choose to pay off the remaining amount of your spending slowly. You can do the same the following month, paying just the minimum sum and rollover the balances. Once you do this, hefty interest charges (from 16% to 24%) will start to apply on rollover balances. The effective interest rate is actually much higher because the interest charges are compounded every month.

This is where the problem starts when people are tempted to spend more than they can afford, accumulating a huge amount of debt as a result.

Many who rely on credit cards for their spending spree without paying the debts incurred in full every month often find themselves on the brink of bankruptcy. When their debts ballooned to such a huge amount, they will soon find it almost impossible to repay. Each time you spend using credit cards with insufficient money to pay in full, you are robbing your future self.

It's in the interest of credit card companies and banks to entice you to use your cards to spend, while hoping that you won't pay off your balances at the end of every month. Because when you don't pay your credit card bills fully, you are granting them the right to charge you the lucrative interest.

Many banks will even organize lucky draws regularly just to entice you to spend more. They will encourage you to increase spending to improve your chances of winning luxurious prizes such as condominiums and fancy cars. But who are the ones paying for those prizes? You are one of them for sure. There is no such thing as a free lunch. Somebody somewhere will be financing those glitzy gifts. Those few prizes will only be won by a few cardholders but the other cardholders will be paying for the prizes. And those with large rollover balances will be bearing the bulk of the costs!

Are You a Compulsive Spender?

The spending disease that affects many people today affect their financial health and cause many people to be perpetually in debt. They see things, want things, and buy things without much considerations about whether they can afford those things or otherwise. So, what if they don't have the cash to buy the things they want now? Just use plastic! Such an unrestrained behavior is the main reason why the businesses of banks and credit card companies are flourishing.

Do you enjoy retail therapy sessions every now and then? My wife and I love shopping. It's one of our favorite pastimes actually. Just like any other thing, shopping, when done in moderation and with restraint, won't be much of a concern. The problem only arises when your shopping spree goes out of control, leading to the piling up of debts. You see things, then want those things, and proceed to buy them without exercising any self-control.

Check and see if the following scenarios apply to you:

- One or more of your credit cards are maxed out.
- You frequently talk to people about things you love to have.
- Your house is getting cluttered with too much stuff.
- You enjoy shopping as a form of retail therapy.
- Payday is equivalent to shopping day.
- You continue to spend despite your mounting debts.
- You keep forgetting how much you spend.
- You hide the things you have bought from your spouse.
- You spend based on your emotions.
- You are constantly reading product reviews and thinking of things to buy.

How many of these scenarios apply to you? If you exhibit more than two of the symptoms listed above, you are likely to be a compulsive spender. Compulsive spending normally starts out small at first, but it could grow into a habit that becomes hard to break. A bit of retail therapy here and there could turn into a frequent and regular activity. This can become an issue if the spending goes out of control. Compulsive spenders rarely plan a budget and habitually spend on non-essential items. They feel they deserve to splurge and give excuses to justify the spending.

Below are some warning signs of an overreliance on credit card, and that your credit isn't managed in a responsible manner:

- Being late in your repayment of mortgage, rent, or car loan.
- Making low or minimum payment on most months.
- Borrowing money to pay your credit card bills.

- Always finding yourself short of cash.
- Using money from one lender to pay another.
- Working a second job to pay bills.
- Applying for another credit card before you have maxed other cards.

Managing your credit responsibly is one life skill you must acquire if you want to secure your financial future. If your credit card debts are piling up, stop using plastic immediately. Only use cash to buy things until all your credit card debts are settled in full. Cut up all your credits cards if you still can't resist the temptations of charging to your cards.

Wealthy people know how to control their spending urges. Whenever there's a need to tighten their belts, they do it without hesitation. They surely won't race to be the first in the long queue during the latest iPhone release. They are probably still using iPhones that are two models behind the latest. That's why the wealthy are few. The fact that Apple has grown to be such a huge company is proof that millions of people worldwide splurged on their grossly overpriced products.

When you see something in the store that you feel a strong urge to buy and somehow believe that you must have it or you'll die, stop at once and delay your purchase. Trust me, you'll live on. Take some time to decide whether the item is a need or merely a want. See if after one week you still have that same strong desire for that item you intended to buy a week ago. Controlling your spending impulses is vital for good stewardship of your money.

Spend Your Income, Not Your Capital

Capital consists of valuable possessions such as houses and retirement funds. It is easy to lose but hard to acquire. Hence, it becomes important to distinguish between money for keeping and money for spending. You should try not to draw down on your capital and try spending on just your income. To people without much assets, all money looks like spending money.

Take for example, my properties are my capital. The rental income derived from my investment properties becomes my income. I will only use the income for my expenditure on consumables. Even though some of my properties has more than doubled in value, I won't be selling any of my properties unless I have plans to use the profits gained from the sale of the property to reinvest in other income-generating assets.

The next time you get a lump sum year-end bonus, try not to spent it immediately on a family holiday or other consumables. Put it away as capital by investing in some bonds, stocks, or any other assets, and watch your capital grow. The profits gained for your investments can then be used as part of your spending money.

Never Overspend

Wealthy people don't overspend. They live by the maxim of spending well below their means. Most of them save at least 20% of their income, living life on the remaining 80%. On the contrary, people who are struggling financially are mostly living above their means. They spend more than they earn and end up with overwhelming debts, causing them sleepless nights.

If you want to end your financial struggles, you must make it a habit to spend within your budget and save the rest. Below are some sensible ways to budget your expenditure that you can use as a general guide:

- Spend no more than 30% of your monthly income on housing loan or rent.
- Spend no more than 10% of your monthly income on motor vehicle loans.
- Spend no more than 15% of your monthly income on groceries.
- Spend no more than 10% of your monthly income on entertainment.
- Spend no more than 5% of your annual income on vacations.

STOP SPENDING MONEY YOU DON'T HAVE

Stay out of credit card debts at all cost. Don't spend future money to buy what you can't afford now. Make it a rule to buy only what you can afford to pay in cash. With the exception of your house and car, never borrow to buy. If your credit card debt is accumulating, it is a clear sign that you are overspending and you'll need to cut back on your expenditures somewhere. Pay off your credit card debts as soon as possible.

I have seen many people going broke because of credit card debts. Many people use credit to indulge in luxury items they can't really afford. It's worth to note that an Omega watch and a Seiko watch will tell the same time; a Louis Vuitton wallet and a Picard wallet will hold the same amount of money; and a Toyota car will bring you to the same destination as a Bentley limousine.

The true value of things isn't reflected on price tags. Similarly, true happiness isn't found in materialistic things. You should have realized that after you indulge in luxurious things, the happy moments will last only for a while before it disappears quickly. Hence, it's not worth incurring debts just to satisfy the short, non-lasting happy moments you may get out of these unnecessary things.

The poor and middle class spend most of their lives working hard for money to buy things that make them appear rich. However, these are mostly unproductive things in the financial sense because these things don't generate income. Frequently, many people buy things they don't need with money they don't have to impress people they don't know. It's unfortunate but it's happening all the time. Such spending habits are the ones that are keeping people from becoming rich.

Many people think that their financial problems would be over if they get a pay increase. This belief ignores the fact that most people live beyond their means. After people receive pay increases, they typically look for ways to improve their lifestyles, resulting in higher living expenses. And they continue to live beyond their means which makes it impossible to experience financial breakthroughs even with increased income. Furthermore, with uncontrollable increase in consumptions without having more income coming into their coffers consistently, wealth can disintegrate in the blink of an eye.

21

Invest to Beat Inflation

Inflation is taxation without legislation.
—Milton Friedman

Are there times when you feel like your dollar doesn't go quite as far as it used to? If that is how you feel, you aren't imagining it. Because it is real. And inflation is the reason. Inflation describes the economic situations where the prices of goods and services increases over time, thus reducing the purchasing value of money. As the general cost of living for the people are impacted due to the increase in prices of goods and services, the appropriate monetary authority of the country, such as the central bank, will then take the necessary measures to keep inflation within permissible limits so as to allow the economy to run smoothly.

Inflation is measured by government indices (expressed as a percentage) in a variety of ways—such as the RPI (Retail Price Index) and the CPI (Consumer Price Index)—depending upon the types of goods and services considered. Both RPI and CPI measure inflation by taking a basket of everyday items that people buy (like food, clothes, petrol, etc.), looking at what they cost the previous last year as compared to now, and finding the proportional difference. However, the CPI exclude the costs of your house such as mortgages, rents, and council tax from the basket. Thus, any increases in housing costs wouldn't be reflected in the CPI. Only the RPI takes into account the costs relating to your house.

Indices indicating price increases of between 0% and 3% per annum are generally acceptable. But persistently high inflation rate of above 5% are bad as it destroys underlying economic incentives and sends wrong signals to investors. The central banks may then try pushing down inflation by pushing up interest rates which could plunge economies into recessions.

The Enemy of Money

The biggest enemy of money is inflation. Although it is true that a penny saved is a penny earned, but due to inflation, the value of the penny saved would be much lesser than when it was earned. You can't ignore the corrosive impact of rising prices on the value of your money. So, if you save your money by storing it under your bed, you'll definitely lose to inflation because the cost of living grows while the value of your money doesn't.

Even if you save your money in a bank account or invest in a Certificate of Deposit (CD), you could still lose to inflation, depending on the interest earned. For example, assuming the average historical rate of inflation at 3%, and you put your cash into a CD earning say 1.4%, you're still losing to inflation by 1.60% (3% less 1.4%). And I have not even factor in the taxes on your savings, which would further reduce your real rate of interest.

There are just too many people who focus just on investment risks alone and ignore the risk of inflation totally. While the need for having a cash cushion can't be stressed enough, the problem is that many people hold much more cash than is needed. They place all or most of their money into bank deposits that give them measly interest income, not knowing that they are sure to lose money over a long period of time.

The table below shows how the real value of $100 are reduced by the impact of inflation:

Impact of inflation on the value of $100			
Number of years	1% inflation rate	3% inflation rate	5% inflation rate
1	$99	$97	$95
3	$97	$92	$86
5	$95	$86	$78
10	$91	$74	$61
20	$82	$55	$38

From the table, we can see that at an inflation rate of 3%, the value of money would be reduced by about 14% in just five years, and about 26% in ten years. Hence, if you don't invest your money to beat inflation, you will be getting poorer as time passes.

With such low saving rates, it really doesn't provide much incentives for investors to hold too much cash because inflation will cause the money to lose its value in real terms. Though your money in the bank is generally safe with little risk, the interest you earned is too little to have any impact on your financial well-being. You should only hold some cash as emergency funds (in case you need money on short notices) and the rest as ammunitions for future investments.

The opportunity cost of holding cash is very high since you will miss out on the chance to invest the money for higher returns. It doesn't make any financial sense to have most of your money kept in the bank when the interest earned won't even beat inflation. Hence, your money in the bank will lose value over time if you don't invest it to earn a higher rate of return.

Investing in stocks, bonds, real estates, or insurance products could yield significantly higher returns. In addition, certain financial products can even provide you with some tax benefits. Why let the tax man take more of your money than is required?

Types of Investments for Beating Inflation

To help mitigate the effects of inflation, you can have your investment portfolio diversified across a number of assets, sectors and geographies. Diversification, though won't ensure gains or guarantee against losses, may provide the potential to improve returns based on your goals, time horizon, and tolerance for volatility.

1. Equities

Investing in equities over a long period is one of the best ways to stay ahead of inflation. Equities provide a powerful way for investors to hedge against inflation because certain good companies have the potential to increase profits in line with inflation. This is because companies are likely to pass on the rising costs to the consumers. Based on this, the company stocks should have a reasonable chance of keeping pace with rising inflation.

Some companies have better opportunity to pass on rising costs than others. For example, companies selling shampoos, toothpaste, laundry detergents, rice, and oil. These are items that most people will continue to buy and use even when these items undergo price increases. Consider allocating some of your money for companies that produce consumer staples by investing in their stocks, which could be paying you good dividends.

2. Properties

Properties have a good track record as a hedge against inflation. Both the prices of properties and rental income would normally increase in line with the inflation rate. The reason is because both the property price and rent are included in the basket of goods and services for the calculation of inflation rate in the retail price index.

Thus, investing in properties provide us a good way to keep up with inflation with the rental income earned and the potential capital appreciation of the properties.

While the historically high returns in the property rental market have almost disappeared in today's economy, property still seems to make good investment sense. In strong property market conditions, landlords will benefit from rising prices and rents.

In a flat economy, any type of property will nevertheless generate a rental income for the landlord. Investors just need to work at cutting rental property expenses to gain better returns.

3. REITs (Real Estate Investment Trusts)

Real Estate Investment Trusts are companies that own or finance income-producing real estate in a range of property sectors such as offices, shopping centers, factories, hospitals and apartment buildings. Real estate has long been a great source of consistent income. This is especially true with REITs owning large diversified portfolios of properties.

The majority of REITs are traded on major stock exchanges. They provide investors a simpler way to invest in real estate other than owning rental properties or flipping houses. REITs operate along a straightforward business model—by leasing space and collecting rent on its real estate, the company generates income which is then paid out to shareholders in the form of dividends. Since REITs are required to distribute at least 90% of their taxable income to shareholders, with most paying out 100%, they tend to offer generous dividends. Averagely, REITS dividends have grown faster than the rate of the inflation. The dividend income, combined with potential price appreciation of REITs, can increase the odds of investors being able to outpace inflation.

4. Gold

Gold is often viewed as a global currency and as a tangible store of value. Physical gold is held by most central banks within the world economy. Many people also view gold as a way to preserve and pass on their wealth from generation to generation. Gold price tends to rise when the cost of living increases as investors have a tendency to turn to this precious metal during inflationary times, causing gold price to go up. Gold also holds its value well in times of geopolitical uncertainties. During such times, gold normally outperforms other types of investment.

People tend to flee to this "crisis commodity" when world tensions rise and when people are losing confidence in their governments.

The role of gold as an inflation hedge is perhaps the most debated and ambiguous issue. Historically, gold can serve as an inflation hedge in the long run, but not in the short run. During bad economic times when paper currencies or fiat currencies can't be trusted, gold will always retain some value. So, although gold isn't a perfect inflation hedge in the short run, it could still be an excellent crisis hedge.

Hence, gold should be viewed as savings for the rainy day and used as a form of financial insurance for your overall investment portfolio. As a guide, you can allocate 5% to 10% of your investment portfolio to gold, depending on your current situation. If you earn a stable income, consider allocating around 5% to gold. Otherwise, invest up to 10% if you don't have regular income.

5. Diversify Internationally

Diversifying your investments globally could assist in making your portfolio more stable and less vulnerable to domestic volatility and inflation. Many domestic companies are diversified internationally. There are also many foreign company stocks or American Depositary Receipts (ADRs) that you can buy in the United States.

In the past, investors may try to reduce domestic market swings on their portfolio returns by investing in other countries. But today, most foreign markets are swinging in tandem. This is due to businesses becoming increasingly global in scale, resulting in financial markets worldwide more closely tied. This also means that what affects one country's financial market will likely affect others as well.

However, international diversification is still beneficial for investors so long as they invest in assets that don't mirror their current portfolio perfectly. All world markets are interrelated; which also means there is a high probability that markets could crash at the same time. However, diversifying internationally take some risks off the table as some countries might still do better than others.

22

Use the 80/20 Rule to Manage More Efficiently

Those who ignore the 80/20 Principle are doomed to average returns. Those who use it must bear the burden of exceptional achievement.
—Richard Koch

If you have studied business or economics in the past, you should be aware of the Pareto Principle. The Pareto Principle (also called the 80/20 Rule) is created by Italian economist and sociologist Vilfredo Pareto. Pareto's original observation was related to population and wealth where he noticed that 80% of Italy's land was owned by 20% of the population. He went on to study other countries and found that a similar distribution pattern applied too. Pareto also investigated various industries and found that interestingly, 80% of production typically came from just 20% of the companies.

The 80/20 Rule states that 80% of outcomes can be attributed to 20% of all causes for any given event. This 80/20 imbalance is also seen in businesses across various industries:

- 80% of total profits is made from 20% of customers.
- 80% of total sales are generated by 20% of salespeople.
- 80% of sales volume is attributed to 20% of products.
- 80% of problems are caused by 20% of employees.
- 80% of software crashes are caused by 20% of bugs.

- 80% of quality problems are caused by 20% of defects.
- 80% of total profits come from 20% of investments.

By understanding the occurrences in business resulting from the 80/20 Rule, managers can identify which operating factors are more crucial and should receive more attention. Knowing that 80% of the consequences stemmed from 20% of the causes, it would make sense for us to focus on the critical 20% of causes so that we can use our limited resources more efficiently.

The 80/20 Rule are not only used in a business environment. It has also been extended for application to other areas like spending habits, investments and wealth distribution.

One important point to note about the Pareto Principle is that the proportion may not always be exactly 80% and 20%, even though the principle suggests that 20% of the input creates 80% of the output in many situations. Inputs and outputs aren't the same thing, and the sum total won't be exactly 100% most of the time. For example, it might not necessarily be 20% of customers that's making up 80% of a company's profits. It could well be that 17% of customers make up 89% of the company's profits instead. Hence, don't get too caught up on the 80/20 proportion or any other numbers. The Pareto Principle could just as easily be called the 88/18 Rule if 88% of the outputs were caused by 18% of the inputs.

The whole idea, most importantly, is that the majority of results were created by a minority of causes. Success is not achieved by doing more. Rather, it is achieved by doing more of what works.

Goal Setting with the 80/20 Rule

Here's how to apply the 80/20 Rule for setting your goals in two simple steps:

1. Write down five goals on a piece of paper.
2. Pick one of the goals that would have the greatest impact on your life.

After completing this exercise, you would have determined the most important goal (or 20% of your goals) that is most valuable to you. You should now spend 80% of your time working at this goal deemed most important.

Don't lose focus on your goal with all the distractions you face daily. Put your energy to work towards achieving your main goal. A study conducted on attitudes of the rich versus the poor in relation to goal setting found that 85% of rich people have one big goal that they work on all the time. Hence, if you want to be rich, do exactly what the wealthy people do. Focus on your own big goal and work at it all the time. I'm certain the outcome will be one that you'll be happy to live with.

Applying the 80/20 Rule to Investing

You want to earn the highest returns possible on your investments, don't you? Yet, not all investments are equal in terms of their returns. One good way is to apply the 80/20 Rule to your investments. Certainly, there are other ways like fundamental analysis, technical analysis, or some candlestick charting techniques; but I don't intend to dwell on these methods in this book.

Note that I'm not suggesting apportioning 80% of your money to stocks and 20% to bonds. We are not applying the 80/20 Rule to the allocation of assets in your investment portfolio. Rather, we are trying to identify the minority of assets that contributes to majority of profits.

Go through all your investments and you may discover that 80% of your returns come from 20% of your holdings. However, the reverse could also be true—20% of your investments are responsible for 80% of your losses. Focus your attention on the 20% of investments that bring in the most profits, or the 20% of investments that lose the most money, depending on what you discover. Figure out your ideal asset allocation based on your risk tolerance, and rebalance your investment portfolio where necessary on a regular basis.

Applying the 80/20 Rule at the Workplace

I'm sure you have encountered people at your workplace who appear busy all day long, and yet they accomplish very little. Why? Two reasons. One reason is that they are just acting busy while doing unproductive things like playing *Clash of Clans* or watching YouTube videos, without anyone noticing what they have been doing. The other could be they are busy working on tasks of low value, while procrastinating on the few that could make real differences to the bottom line of companies or even their own career developments.

Each day before you start work, ask yourself: "Is this task in the top 20% of my activities for the day that I should be spending 80% of my energy doing it?" The high-impact tasks are frequently the hardest to do, and they're those that most people would have a tendency to avoid. However, the rewards for completing them are often the greatest.

We need to make conscious efforts to resist the temptation of always working on simple and low-value tasks first. Otherwise, we will end up with the habit of always clearing the work at the bottom 80% of all tasks. Prioritizing our time and energy to complete the lower-value tasks first will render us less effective as well as yielding lower results.

23

Get Rich Quick and Go Broke Fast

Greed is the lack of confidence of one's own ability to create.
—Vanna Bonta

Knowledge is power. The more you know, the better off you can be in life. I couldn't agree more. If you are a newbie who is on the lookout for opportunities to create wealth, you will likely be bombarded by many scams promising little risk and fast results. You probably won't be able to tell the difference between a get-rich-quick scheme and a genuine business opportunity. If you aim to get rich quick by choosing the easy way out, you're likely to go broke fast. You risk financial and emotional devastation, together with wasted time, energy and other resources.

Luck has very little to do with becoming wealthy. It takes wisdom, discipline and patience to build wealth, and keep wealth. A savvy investor's ability to recognize and capitalize on a good investment opportunity isn't by chance or coincidence. It requires knowledge, skills and a lot of research work.

Building wealth is often a slow process. Chasing after quick riches is an exercise in futility. The media frequently promote the idea that getting rich quick is simple and easily achieved. But sorry to disappoint you, the allure of fast and easy money is a mirage. It's impossible, always has been, and always will be.

All get-rich-quick schemes being offered are scams. Swindlers who pretend to invest the money of their victims are still doing brisk businesses. Like spotting a diamond among rocks, the ability to sniff out a scam among genuine business opportunities, and to identify a fraudster among honest entrepreneurs, require skills, experience and diligence. You must read, study, research and ask questions. Experiencing the highs and lows of managing your money will also help you gain the wisdom and required skills to become wealthy. You must be willing to learn from the wealthy if you desire financial success for there's much wisdom to be gained from them.

Why Do People Fall for Scams?

Time and time again, stories of people falling victims to get-rich-quick scams keep emerging. Many people simply can't resist searching for easy ways to avoid work and go straight to riches, making themselves easy targets for fraudsters. Even the purportedly smart and successful people aren't spared, as in the case of the Bernie Madoff multibillion-dollar Ponzi scheme. Do you know why? The truth lies in 2 words: fear and greed.

The fear of not having enough makes one greedy, which in turn makes the individual vulnerable to fraud. Every time a recession hits, many scams and bogus investment opportunities surface. Similarly, when the stock market turns from bull to bear, investors become worried and fear sets in, with some falling prey to scam artists offering schemes promising unbelievable returns on their investments. These scam artists are masterful at presenting seemingly legitimate investment schemes. They aim to gain your trust so much so that you'll be willing to hand over your cash to them; and expecting to get the promised high returns on your investments in the not-too-distant future.

Greed has a way of entering your life and causing you to do stupid things with your resources. It will lead you right into the hands of scammers, intent on taking your hard-earned money, if you succumbed to the temptation of easy money within a short time frame. Never let greed blocks your path to prosperity.

The Bernie Madoff $65 Billion Scam

Bernie Madoff was a former non-executive chairman of the Nasdaq stock market and served on the board of directors of the Securities Industry Association. He was also a founding board member of the International Securities Clearing Corporation. Madoff was a respected figure on Wall Street until his multibillion-dollar Ponzi scheme collapsed, resulting in investors suffering heavy losses. He spent the money from his clients on family and friends, rather than investing it, and then took in more money from additional investors to pay out early investors to cover up the fraud.

On December 10, 2008, Madoff confessed to senior employees of his company that the advisory business was actually a fraud and a giant Ponzi scheme. He said the business had lost about $50 billion and that he plans to turn himself in to authorities in a week. Madoff was arrested the next day for operating a multibillion-dollar Ponzi scheme from his investment advisory business.

How did Madoff's clients fall for his $65 billion scam? How could so many rich and successful people become so spectacularly gullible? Madoff had hundreds of victims who were acquainted with him through country clubs and social networks. There were also charities, benefactors and celebrities including Steven Spielberg, John Malkovich, Kevin Bacon, Kyra Sedgwick, Larry King, Pedro Almodóvar and Fred Wilpon among others. Most of Madoff's victims were not financial experts and he abused their trust and used the money to finance his lavished lifestyle.

Scam rarely has a silver lining, but at the very least you can try to draw some lessons from the mistakes of others. Low risk and high return investments are extremely rare, and such high profit outcomes are low probability.

You can outsource anything, but never ever outsource your thinking. Allowing others to do your thinking is dangerous and unwise. Do your own due diligence and don't rely on financial advisors, consultants, stock brokers or economists to do the thinking for you.

Don't invest in anything you can't understand. You need to know what exactly you're investing in if you want to reduce the risks of losing your capital. If at any point in time you are skeptical about an investment; or if something seems fishy; or you feel something isn't quite right about the person recommending the investment proposal; drop the investment immediately.

There is no easy way out as far as wealth creation is concerned. It is your money, your retirement, and your responsibility. You will be on your own managing your own money most of the time. So, don't expect much help from other people. The truth is, nobody cares about your money more than you do.

Get-Rich-Quick Schemes to Look Out For

There are lots of get-rich-quick schemes out there preying on unsuspecting innocent people and newbie investors. Following are some of the more common ones that you need to be aware of.

1. High-Yield Investments

In such investment schemes, investors are promised high returns on a no (or low risk) and high yield guarantee plan. Here's an investment truth you must know—a combination of high-return and low-risk investment schemes rarely exist in this world. Please don't be convinced by people trying to offer you these "low risk" deals. Flee from them instead. It's worth mentioning again—never invest in anything you don't fully understand.

2. Ponzi Schemes

The name originated with Charles Ponzi, who promised 50% returns on investments in only 90 days. Ponzi schemes are based on fraudulent investment management services where money is collected from later investors to pay early investors. Basically, investors contribute funds to the "portfolio manager" who promises clients a high investment return. When investors want their money back, the firm will pay them with the incoming money contributed by later investors. The company controls the entire operation and merely transfer money from one investor to another without any real investment activities with the funds contributed by investors.

Ponzi schemes will flourish so long as new investors continue joining to finance the system, where their funds are used to keep paying those investors who got in earlier. Such schemes are not sustainable in the long run and will eventually collapse when:

- It becomes hard to recruit new investors which also means the cash inflow will cease;
- Too many existing investors start to withdraw and request for their investment returns;
- The scheme operator takes the remaining investment funds and runs.

Therefore, don't be attracted to such schemes by simply looking at their unbelievably high investment returns. Never in my life have I come across any great opportunity that doesn't require thinking, planning and efforts. The bottom line is, if anything sounds too good to be true, it probably is!

3. Pyramid Schemes

Pyramid schemes have existed for at least a century in different guises. This business model pays people for recruiting members into the scheme, rather than products or services. Its members are paid solely by recruiting people into the company.

In a pyramid scheme, there is little or no emphasis on the sale of any products or services. Such schemes only funnel the recruitment money collected to the members high up in the pyramid. Those who get in early and who are placed at the top of the pyramid win while everybody else loses. Characteristics of such business model makes pyramid schemes illegal and unsustainable in the long-run.

Many people confuse pyramid schemes with the legitimate multi-level marketing (or network marketing) businesses. On the surface, pyramid schemes and network marketing businesses appear to share similar traits. On a closer look, however, significant differences exist that make pyramid schemes illegal in most countries.

Network marketing business opportunities always involve the actual selling of products, whereas pyramid schemes don't. The compensation plan is often based on the training and management of team members. In a legitimate network marketing business, the individual business owners are paid only when products are purchased or sold, and no commissions will be paid for the recruitment of new members.

4. Business-in-a-Box Opportunities

If you are in the process of searching for business ideas, chances are you will come across many business-in-a-box opportunities. The business pitch goes something like this: "For only XXXX dollars (amount of money varies from company to company), you can start your own business right away! We'll provide you with the website, products, marketing materials, plus all the training you'll ever need!" Wow, that sure sounds like a fantastic deal, isn't it?

The harsh reality is that thousands of people are falling victim to fraudsters peddling business-in-a-box opportunities presented in many attractive forms. These businesses usually promise financial freedom through work-at-home scams, pyramid schemes masked under network marketing businesses, and a variety of bogus business franchises. These unscrupulous scamming companies only care about making money by preying on gullible and unsuspecting people who are looking for ways to earn some extra income.

Think about it for a moment. The company selling you this business concept will also be offering the same package deal to everyone else. That means thousands of people who took up the deal would be selling the same products, featuring the same website, and using the same marketing strategies as you. You literally face thousands of identical competitors, all without any differentiation whatsoever. Do you think you can win with such a business concept? To me, the whole idea of the business-in-a-box concept is broken at the fundamental level. If you don't already know how to run a business, how is it easy to know what to do with the things in the "box"? Furthermore, if the products are really that fantastic, why aren't they selling the products themselves instead of just selling the business packages to others?

Business-in-a-box is just a bunch of stuff that has been marketed thousands of times. There are really no legitimate reasons why such concept can work for you in the long-run.

5. Affinity Fraud

An affinity fraud is a form of investment scam in which the fraudster targets members of an identifiable group based on religion, race, age, language, or profession. The con artist could be a member of the group, or pretends to be one, and frequently promoting a Ponzi or pyramid scheme to members of the community.

Affinity fraud is perhaps the most subtle and insidious form of scam, exploiting the inherent trust and friendship within group members. A common method used by the con artist is enlisting respected leaders from within the group to spread the word about the fraudulent scheme. The leaders, who may not even know that the investment scheme is actually a scam, might innocently promote the fraudulent investments to their members, who look up to their leaders with much respect. For example, the fraudster may target the church congregation by enlisting the help of pastors to market the fraudulent investment scheme, thus making the church leaders unwitting pawns or victims of the scam.

Keep Your Investments Simple

Investments need not be complicated. The average investor should never engage a complex way to make money. They should understand how their money is being invested before putting in the capital to invest. Keeping your investment portfolio simple is actually the most sophisticated way to manage your money.

Confusion is a fraudster's best friend. Many people would just invest in anything even if they don't understand what they are investing in, so long as they are promised good profits. Don't be fooled. There are so many con artists operating everywhere in this world for a simple reason—the market is BIG. Why is there such a huge market for the scammers to operate successfully? It is because there are simply too many greedy fools around! A fool and his money are soon parted.

If you don't understand how your money will make you more money in an investment scheme, you shouldn't be putting your money into it. Never listen and yield to the promise of high investment returns alone, no matter how good they may sound. Consider other investment alternatives that you understand instead. Before signing up for any business opportunities, do your own due diligence and conduct some research to find out more about the companies offering the schemes. Check out the federal agencies or relevant government authorities that could provide information about phony as well as legitimate business opportunities. Most importantly, guard yourself against greed if you desire to prosper. And always remember that there is no such thing as quick and easy money.

24

Health is Wealth

It is health which is real wealth, and not pieces of gold and silver.
—Mahatma Gandhi

Money and health are two elements of the vicious cycle—the lack of money causes much stress, prolonged stress can cause health problems, and health problems can lead to more financial struggles. The popular proverb telling us that "health is wealth" is surely worth noting and taken seriously in the way we live our lives.

A lot of people are suffering from obesity, high cholesterol, high blood pressure, diabetes, heart diseases, and many other health-related problems. Many of these health issues occur mostly because of how people live their lives. An individual's lifestyle matters a lot and it's directly related to the person's health.

You need health to make money. Don't you think it is hard for you to make money from a hospital bed? Therefore, if you want to be wealthy, you must to take care of your health too. Staying healthy isn't difficult. It merely involves some lifestyle changes. Regular exercise and healthy eating habits are all we need to undertake to gain optimal health.

Fitness is one area where many people don't put much emphasis in their day-to-day living until sicknesses befall. People easily say to themselves, "I'm too busy, too tired, too weak, too lazy, too whatever, to exercise today. And I shall surely do it tomorrow, next week, next month, next year, next time." But the time for you to start exercising never seems to come. Valid reasons or mere excuses? You decide. Interestingly, a study found that people who don't exercise lost about seven years of life compared to those who did. Surely, seven more years would give your investments some more time to grow and add to your net worth!

A person with poor health can't enjoy the pleasure of being wealthy. It is pointless to have all the money in the world and yet don't have good health to enjoy what money can buy. Imagine yourself walking into a luxurious five-star hotel but can't eat a sumptuous meal with your loved ones because of health issues. Or you can't enjoy a drink with your friends once in a while simply because you over-did drinking during your younger days. Staying healthy therefore becomes a necessity for everybody. We need to develop and maintain lifelong plans to manage not only our money, but our health too.

Ways to Stay Healthy

Living a healthy lifestyle doesn't mean you have to eat only vegetables and spend hours working out at the gym every single day. It is about making manageable healthy choices in your daily living. A healthy lifestyle is fairly straightforward—eat right; exercise regularly; manage stress; avoid smoking; limit consumption of fatty foods, salt, sugar and alcohol; and get enough sleep like seven to eight hours. Below are ten essential tips that will help us stay fit and healthy:

1. Find Time to Exercise

Former U.S. President Barack Obama works out 45 minutes a day, six days a week. In his autobiography *Dreams From My Father*, Obama admitted to being a casual drug user and underachiever until he started running three miles a day. He was also known to play basketball on courts in federal buildings around Washington when he was President. Today, he continues to stick to his combination of strength and cardio workout routine.

The human body is designed to move—walk, run, jump, squat, bend, stretch, etc. Movement is what prevents the body from breaking down. However, with today's technological advancements, the need for body movements decreases significantly. People now drive cars everywhere they go; spend long hours sitting at their desks during work; and entertain themselves while sitting in couches watching TV, playing video games, or fiddling with their gadgets. Exercise, therefore, functions to fill the gap between our decreased daily physical activities and the body's natural need for movements to remain fit and healthy.

Exercise is crucial and is a must to remain fit and healthy. It improves your health, fight diseases and help you hone life skills such as confidence and persistence. Any form of physical activity is good for us. Some health benefits can be achieved from as little as 60 minutes of moderate-intensity aerobic activity per week, though ideally, we should have at least 150 minutes of moderate-intensity per week, or 75 minutes of high-intensity workouts per week. Activities such as walking, jogging, aerobics and workouts in the gym will help regulate your heart rate, so you will have more energy for your activities through the day.

Exercise is an effective way to boost your health and keep your energy flowing at optimum levels throughout the day. Getting some exercise done early in the morning won't make you feel lazy in the day. It helps improves blood circulation and releases muscle tension, giving you a stronger body and mind.

There is no need for any exercise equipment if you don't have any access to a gym. Body exercise routines like pushups, crunches, lunges, squats, jumping jacks, or planks can be done at home or other places easily. These simple body exercises are as effective as working out in the gym, and can go a long way in building your health.

Start exercising today, because one day you may want to, but won't be able to. So, don't procrastinate any further and just do it. You must take good care of your body now so that it can take care of you for the rest of your life!

2. Never Remain Seated for Long Hours

Most office workers remain seated for many hours each day at their workstations. Many spend long hours behind their computers. Sitting for long hours without much movements will slow down metabolism and weaken muscles. Make sure you get up and move around every hour. Walk around often and stretch your muscles from time to time. Set a timer to remind you hourly to do so.

3. Don't Eat Mindlessly

It is common to see many people eating round-the-clock these days. Eating seems to be people's favorite pastime. People nowadays don't eat only when they're hungry—they eat when they're bored, they eat when they're happy, they eat when they're sad, they eat when they're angry, and they eat for whatever reasons they have. We need to learn to avoid mindless eating and drinking unless we plan to shift our place of residence to a hospital.

In a gathering with friends over a buffet meal one evening, one of my friends jokingly exclaimed, "Let us eat, drink and be merry, for tomorrow we *diet*." We all laughed, somewhat in agreement, but knowing in our hearts that we didn't plan to diet after the feast. My friend's words, which was tweaked, was lifted from the Scriptures (Isaiah 22:13) where the original word is "die" instead of "diet." But it can really do harm to our body and our health if we live by my friend's joke. How many people are mindful of what food or the amount of food they eat every day? Judging by the number of overweight people we have around us, the answer is probably not many. No wonder so many people in affluent countries are experiencing lifestyle diseases—obesity, heart disease, type 2 diabetes, stroke, and cancer—owing to their daily eating habits and the way they live their lives. Granted, we are likely to be overeating every now and then due to entertaining friends or business associates, attending functions, celebrating special occasions with loved ones over buffet meals, but overeating on a continual basis can be dangerous.

If you are someone taking supper regularly, it's time to reconsider your late-night eating habits. Regular or frequent late-night supper can sabotage your health. Dining right before you sleep may elevate your heart disease risk. In addition, late-night supper could cause acid reflux and indigestion, which interferes with your sleep. Eating meals on time is as important as having a healthy meal. Consuming food at least two hours before you hit the bed prevent obesity and other severe health complications.

4. Eat More Healthy Food and Avoid the Unhealthy Ones

Unhealthy diets are mostly high in calories. Avoid them whenever possible. Unhealthy food will gradually take a toll on your health, leading to weight gain, heart diseases and cholesterol. Eat a lot of fruits and vegetables that are rich in fibers, vitamins and other good nutrients.

Eat a proper meal whenever possible only when you are hungry. Your stomach isn't a rubbish to dump your junk cravings. Eat only when necessary and also ensure the food is wholesome and healthy. A good nutrition guideline calls for eating a variety of fruits and vegetables; whole grains; wide protein sources including lean meats, eggs, legumes, beans and nuts; and healthy high-fat foods such as avocado and olive oil.

As far as possible, try to reduce consumption of sugar and salt; food containing saturated fats and trans fats; and refined grains. Consuming excessive sugar, salt and fats can increase the risks of obesity, heart disease and other health problems. A little indulgence of ice-cream and your favorite cheesecake are fine once in a while, but don't make sinful desserts a ritual in every meal. Exercise self-control and eat everything in moderation.

People all over the world are also consuming refined white flour much more these days. Refined white flour is stripped of almost all fiber, vitamins and minerals and thus provide little nutritional value. This is because the hull, which is the fibrous and nutritious part of the grain, is being removed during the refining process. Whole grains, on the other hand, are prepared using the entire grain including the hull. Hence, whole-grains food products provide us better nutrition. Try switching from white bread and white rice to whole-meal bread and brown rice for better nutritional values.

5. Have a Balanced Diet

A balanced diet is one that gives your body the nutrients it needs to function correctly. Incorporating proteins, minerals, iron, vitamins, calcium, carbohydrates and some fats (good fats like monounsaturated fat and polyunsaturated fat) in your daily diet is essential for good health. Fruits, vegetables, lean meat, poultry, and whole grain foods make a balanced diet. A balanced diet is very important because your body needs proper nutrition to work effectively. Without good nutrition, your body is more prone to disease, infection and fatigue.

6. Don't Smoke

Every cigarette you smoke is harmful to your body and can cause fatal diseases such as lung cancer, pneumonia and emphysema. Smoking narrows the arteries, making it harder for blood to flow. It also increases blood pressure and heart rate. Avoid smoking as it will ruin your health sooner or later.

Secondhand smoke, also known as passive smoke, is tobacco smoke that's exhaled by a smoker, or is given off by burning tobacco (or cigarette), and inhaled by people nearby. Passive smoke is bad for your health because it has the same harmful chemicals that smokers inhale and it can cause cancer too.

As there is no safe level of exposure for secondhand smoke, try to avoid getting too close to smokers so that you won't inhale the harmful chemicals.

7. Drink Sufficient Water

Staying hydrated is important since about 60% of the adult human body is water. As we are losing water constantly from our body via urine and sweat, we need to drink adequate amounts of water to prevent our bodies from dehydration.

Drink at least eight glasses of water every day. If weather is hot, or you exercise a lot and perspire much, drink an additional two to three glasses of water to stay hydrated. Drinking water helps flushes your system and keeps your skin good and healthy too.

8. Limit Alcohol Consumption

Many people swear that a little alcohol is good for health. Drinking may also help you relax after a hard day's work. However, there are experts who insist that the safest amount of alcohol to consume is none at all!

Alcohol, scientifically a neurotoxin and a cardiotoxin, injures the person's pancreas and immune system which leads an increase in risk of cancers. Drinking too much alcohol reduces the number of white blood cells that helps the body fights germs, making your body a much easier target for diseases. Chronic drinkers are also more liable to contract diseases like pneumonia and tuberculosis than moderate drinkers.

While no one should pick up drinking in search of better health, moderate drinking of up to a glass per day probably won't hurt anybody.

9. Get Sufficient Sleep

Nearly two-thirds of Americans say they lose sleep due to stress. That is especially unfortunate because sleep helps fight against some of the fallout of stress. The human body is a machine. And just like any machine requires rest and recharging, our bodies also need sufficient sleep to rejuvenate. Many people, burdened by the monotony of work, tend to sleep less and focus more on their tasks. But the thing is, you can't really focus if you haven't had a good night's sleep. Adequate sleep increases your productivity and helps you get tasks done more efficiently.

Having poor sleep regularly has also been linked to health issues including:

- Impaired memory
- Reduced immune defenses
- Increased risk of cancer and heart disease
- Increased risk of depression and anxiety
- Weight gain

In order to maintain good health, getting sufficient sleep is as important as eating healthily and exercising. Sleeping relaxes your mind and keeps you healthy. Get seven to eight hours sleep every night. You simply cannot achieve optimal health without taking care of your sleep.

10. Avoid Pessimistic Thinking

Pessimistic thinking is one of the most poisonous drugs known to humanity. Pessimists have a tendency to incline towards negativity and they expect the worst in most situations. Besides taking a toll on their mental health, their physical health could be affected too.

Pessimism is associated with anxiety, depression, sleep disorders, high blood pressure and lifestyle choices that are damaging to a person's overall health and well-being. The irony is that pessimism is self-induced. Negative people are so habituated to their pessimistic thinking patterns that they rarely realize it's destructive to their lives. Developing an optimistic attitude can alter your life in amazing ways. The situation and things around you aren't as bad as they seem to be—it is your mind that is playing the dirty trick most of the time.

Health Lets You Live Life Fully

Health is a state of complete physical, emotional and social well-being. It is a resource that allows a person to live a full life. Let's be honest and admit it. You only appreciate the real value of your health after it's lost. In the absence of health, you'll come to understand how tough life can be without it when you need to fight those never-ending health problems. Every time you get sick, you act out of fear to do things so your illness don't get worse. But as soon as you get well, your lifestyle goes back to what it was before, without any extra effort to maintain optimal health. That's very true, isn't it? It was true for me at least. It was when I was immobilized for four days due to a back injury that got me worried about my health again.

At just 1.65 meters tall, I used to weigh about 77 kilograms with a waistline of 36 inches. With a body mass index (BMI) of 28.3, which is a measure of body fat based on height and weight, I was classified as overweight then. Not excessively obese but certainly not in a good physical state, and shape, either. My blood pressure and cholesterol levels were high too.

After my back injury, I spent most of the time lying in bed for those four days, and it got me motivated and determined to get my fitness level, body physique and health back on track. I sprang into action immediately after I recovered. And you know what?

My weight went down to 63 kilograms and my waistline was reduced to 29 inches in just three months! My BMI was also down to a healthy 23.1 resulting from the loss of 14 kilograms.

Do you want to know how I achieve such amazing result? I'm sure you do! Now, here's the secret: I took a magic pill every day without fail. This daily magic pill consists of—walking about 23 kilometers (about 30,000 steps); doing about 45 minutes of body exercises; watching what I eat; drinking sufficient water; and stopping my habit of eating supper. That's all. Basically, I adhered to the healthy tips that I shared earlier on a daily basis.

Today, my blood pressure is back to normal and I don't have cholesterol issues anymore. I continue my routine of walking at least 20,000 steps a day, do daily body exercises, and diligently follow those health tips. I'm back in great health with a better physical shape. My wife, inspired by my determination to get back in shape, followed my daily routine and she has achieved a weight loss of ten kilograms in three months. Besides regaining my health, I also gain a committed partner living a healthy lifestyle together!

You don't have to spend thousands of dollars at weight loss centers or popping slimming pills. You just need to put in some effort with a generous dose of discipline, and an unwavering commitment to eat healthier, exercise, and remove any bad lifestyle habits to enjoy good health. It's simple, but certainly not easy. However, the end result and health benefits would be well worth the time and effort.

Besides ensuring you have a good financial health, you must also work at your long-term physical health. Good health enables you to thrive and reach your full potential. The loss of health is a loss of all happiness and success. Healthy living is a lifestyle and not a short-term goal. As nothing is more valuable than good health, prize your health above everything else.

PART FOUR

SHARE YOUR RICHES

No one has ever become poor by giving.
—Anne Frank

You have worked so hard and burnt the midnight oil to earn your riches. Doesn't it sound really unfair to suggest that you share your riches with others? In your mind, you may be thinking: "Why should I share my wealth with people who never put in the same effort like I do?" Yes, you absolutely have a valid point here. It seems there isn't any good reason why you should give away any of your hard-earned money.

However, I'm not talking about sharing riches with those self-indulgent and lazy people, who don't work hard for their living, but simply stretching out their hands waiting to receive from others. Rather, I'm referring to people who are less fortunate, the needy, and the deserving. It's always good to share good things with others. Sharing is caring.

Most of us live in comfortable homes, have enough to eat, and never face problems putting three meals on the table. Our children also have warm clothes to wear in cold weather, and many toys to play with. And yet, there are many poor people in our country, and around the world, who are living in poverty and barely surviving. We pass by some of these poor people on the streets we walk each day. Others are living in shelters or the margins in substandard housing. There are enough opportunities for us to offer a helping hand.

Our natural instinct is to hoard our resources, in case we need a little extra some day in the future. However, we shouldn't be preoccupied only with how to acquire wealth to benefit only ourselves, but also with how to share our riches with others. We have an obligation to help the poor and be a channel of provision for those who can't meet their basic needs.

Although we can't solve everybody's problem, we shouldn't stop doing what we are able to. Whenever we are in a position to help someone, we should. We need to be generous and give for the sake of making the world a better place for all of us to live in. Generosity not only benefits the receiver; it also rewards the giver.

Winston Churchill, one of the greatest, statesmen of the 20th century, said it right: "We make a living by what we get, but we make a life by what we give." We are all going to get to a certain level where enough is going to be enough. Give everything else away. Besides, giving back to society makes life richer!

25

Be a Blessing to Others

Not he who has much is rich, but he who gives much.
—Erich Fromm,

The Dead Sea is a gigantic salt lake in Israel. At 304 meters (997 feet) deep, it's the deepest hypersaline lake in the world. And with a salinity of 342 grams per kilogram, or 34.2%, the Dead Sea is almost ten times as salty as the ocean. There are no fishes, plants, or any other visible life in the lake. Anyone accidentally swallowing the water while swimming or diving could even lead to asphyxiation (dying of suffocation due to the lack of oxygen)!

Why is the Dead Sea so dead? The reason is because the Dead Sea is a terminus for the flow of water and rain—water flows into it but doesn't flow out. The Jordan River flows through the Great Rift Valley and eventually empties into the Dead Sea, where its water has no escape. The flow stops completely at the Dead Sea, and so does its life. In other words, the Dead Sea receives but it doesn't give.

We can surely learn a great lesson about life here. Life isn't only about receiving, but giving as well. It is a privilege to give, and we truly live when we give.

I heard of a story where an African boy was rescued from a famine-hit area. A rescue-worker observed that the boy, when given bread to eat, would always consume only half the bread, keeping the other half for the next day. This African boy has grown up in an environment with scarcity of food that he treasures food with his life.

What about us? For most of us, it isn't a case of whether there is bread on the table or not. It is whether the bread comes with bacon or tuna. I have witnessed so many children, sometimes adults even, eating only half their food and wasting the other half. Indeed, how bless they are to be in excess and able to put food to waste! Whenever we are tempted to waste any food, just pause for a moment to think about the starving people who crave to eat your unwanted food. With excess resources, why not think about how to bless others instead?

Exercise Control over Money

Many people, after becoming rich, don't really have total control over their money. They upgrade their houses, live posh lifestyles and buy luxury items. But when it comes to helping the needy, these rich people turn a blind eye. They find it hard to let go of their money, and have become enslaved to money instead of being masters over money. What's the outcome? The rich who don't bless others will become selfish and lonely people.

The following story comes to my mind...

There is a village that is infested with so many monkeys that it started to cause problems to the local villagers and farmers. The monkeys not only started to eat fruits from the fruit trees, but also steal food from people's house. It got so bad that something had to be done. A gathering among the villagers was held to discuss what can be done about the problem. A wise man then came forward and declared to the villagers, "I've got a great idea to catch those monkeys. Leave it to me!"

The next day, the wise man went out to execute his idea. He drilled a small hole on the side of a coconut, drained out the coconut water, filled a third of it with peanuts and then place it near a tree those monkeys frequently visit to eat the fruits. A short while later, a monkey came near the coconut and reached down the small hole of the coconut to grab those peanuts.

When trying to extract the peanuts, the monkey found that its clenched fist full of peanuts won't get through the narrow opening of the coconut. The villagers came and chased after the monkey. The fearful monkey, with only one free hand and another trapped inside a coconut, wouldn't want to let go of the peanuts to escape from the villagers. Eventually, the monkey was caught and killed by the villagers.

It's obvious to us—the only way the monkey can escape from the villagers is to let go of the peanuts to free its hand from the coconut. With both hands free, the monkey would then be able to climb up the tree to save its life. But the monkey didn't do that. It just couldn't let go and wouldn't want to. Hence the tragic outcome for the monkey.

Think for a moment. Have we been holding on to peanuts that we can't let go? Are we hanging on to something so tightly that we imprison ourselves? Are we able to let go of the things holding us back to gain back our freedom? It's really up to us. And only we can decide our own destinies.

Let's stop the urge to grab and grab in the pursuit of wealth. Start contributing to society through our giving, and in whatever ways we can. We must learn to let go and release our resources to bless others.

Give and It Shall Be Given Unto You

The more you give, the more you receive. This is one incredible universal truth that has stood the test of time. It's virtually a law of nature, not just a religious doctrine. Be generous and give, and it shall be given unto you. Yes, you will be given back in more ways than you'll ever know. It's an indisputable law—you reap what you sow and you get back what you put in. You get to see evidence of this law in your daily living. When you get angry at people, they get angry at you. When you treat others with respect, you get treated with respect in return. If you are courteous to others, they will be courteous to you. If you are generous to people, people will be generous to you. See the point?

It's strange that when it comes to money, many people hesitate in believing that this law is still applicable. They become less inclined to bless others with their money, whether to a charity, or any other worthy causes. They seem to believe that their money will be gone the moment it's given away, and that they'll never get their money back. It's a mentality of fear, greed, selfishness, hoarding, lack, or whatever you like to call it. In other words, it's a scarcity mindset. There are also those who believe that you must be ruthless in order to be rich and successful. They couldn't be more wrong! Wealthy people hardly possess such thinking and mentality because they operate with an abundance mindset. The wealthy believe there will always be new opportunities to make more money and get further ahead in life.

Learn to give, give more, and keep giving. Giving to others ultimately puts a smile on your face. You will eventually discover that giving does more for you than the person receiving your gift.

Make a Difference in the Life of Others

Have you ever wondered whether you can truly make a difference to the lives of other people? Yes, you surely can. The blessings you received in your life will enable you to make a difference to the lives of those around you.

Once you become rich or have reached a comfortable level in your life, consider making a difference in someone else's life instead of spending more time and effort to amass more wealth. Warren Buffett donated $30 billion towards the Bill & Melinda Gates Foundation's goals to prevent childhood deaths, end diseases, and improve the lives of people worldwide. He is also committed to donating more that 99% of his wealth to charity during his lifetime or at the time of his death.

Now, I can almost hear you say, "If I'm a billionaire like Warren Buffett, I'll be willing to donate billions of dollars to help the poor too!" But let me put it this way—if you are not willing to give hundreds from the thousands (or even tens of thousands) you are earning right now, don't expect it to become easier if you have millions, or even billions. I bet you won't suddenly become enlightened once you get wealthy. Similarly, having more riches won't cause you to immediately develop a sense of righteousness to want to help the less fortunate. It starts with what you already have now, not what you'll be having tomorrow.

Sharing Is Caring

I believe sharing all things (with the exception of your spouse of course) with others would lead to an enriching life. Riches are like manure, which stinks in a heap, but if spread, makes the earth fruitful and plants will grow. Very true, isn't it? If you are wealthy, learn also to give back. It blesses your soul. Even if you are not rich, you can give in other ways too. Giving back doesn't have to be limited to money—it can include your time, talent, expertise, and things you own as well.

If you are going to give, just give. Give freely and willingly, especially to the people who can't give back to you. You don't need anything in return. And don't expect anything in return too. Donating funds or giving away new or used goods to the less fortunate can go a long way. What may be little to you, may be everything to another. And what may be trash to you, may be someone else's treasure. Hence, never let the size of your gift keeps you from giving. It is more important that you give from your heart, without expecting anything in return. Volunteers are also needed in places like orphanages, senior citizen homes, homeless shelters, etc.

We can bless others in many ways. Some examples include giving material gifts, donating to charities, giving your time to volunteer, valuing others, saying kind words, and offering encouragement and support. Maybe you know or come across someone with a financial problem that is not caused by any financial mismanagement? Offer a listening ear, together with a love gift of money if you're able to. Or maybe your friend who has been laid off but couldn't find employment for a long period of time? Offer encouragement and take your friend out for meals. Our greatness isn't what we have, it is what we give.

If you sincerely bless others in every given opportunity, such kind of genuine generosity tend to spill over to other areas of your life. You will become more generous with your time, words, and actions toward your family, friends, colleagues and others.

The happiest people are often not those receiving more, but those giving more. God's blessings to us are not meant to end with us. His desire is that the blessings filter down to others in need. We are blessed so we can be a blessing to others.

Let us choose to consume a little less and contribute a little more. This will result in making our lives much more fulfilling. If we can live simply and give, others can receive and simply live!

26

Don't Be a Money Lender

Money lent to a friend must be recovered from an enemy.
—German Proverb

"Neither a borrower nor a lender be" is a famous phrase said by Polonius, chief counselor to King Claudius, in Act I, Scene III of William Shakespeare's play, *Hamlet*. As Polonius gives some fatherly advice to his son Laertes, Shakespeare provided us a great timeless advice: Do not lend money to a friend, and do not borrow money from a friend.

So, why are we advised not to lend money to friends?

Polonius answered the question in his next line, "For loan oft loses both itself and friend." You see, Polonius knew that a loan to a friend, or even a family member, often results in the loss of both the money and the relationship.

It is also wise for us to make it a rule not to borrow money from friends and relatives as well. Why? Because if you fail to pay them back on time, or at all, you risk losing the relationship in which you may value more than the money itself.

The only exception I can think of is when your friends or relatives wish to put money into a business that you are planning to start up. If this is the case, the money would be considered as an investment rather than a loan. The lender could then be entitled to partial ownership of the business entity, and permitted to collect dividends at the appropriate time.

What to Do If People Approach You to Borrow Money

The most important principle you must adhere to is this: never ever borrow money from anyone, including money lending institutions, to help others. You shouldn't loan any money you don't have under any circumstances. Otherwise, you could land yourself into potential financial troubles in the future should you be unable to pay back the loan to your lender.

Following are three basic guidelines of lending money:

1. Make it a policy to say "no" to borrowers.
2. Offer help in other nonmonetary ways.
3. Make the loan in writing if you must lend for some reasons.

Try your best to avoid the third guideline as far as possible, for reasons already mentioned earlier. If you really value the relationship with the borrower, don't lend any money.

1. Saying "No"

Most of us have trouble saying "no" to people for a simple reason—we prefer others to perceive us as nice people. I had my own encounters where long-lost friends called me suddenly out of nowhere with the intention to borrow money. I struggled at first, even lending money in the first few instances. As more of such loan requests from friends surfaced, I started to reject them. For those that I have lent money to initially, I never recovered my money, and the relationships with those friends were no more. The warning by William Shakespeare—not to lend or borrow money from friends because you could lose both—is thus wise and sensible. And I have learned my lesson.

DON'T BE A MONEY LENDER

You can say "no" to people in many different ways. Try rejecting them with statements like:

- "Sorry, it is my policy not to loan any money to people."
- "Sorry, I don't have excess funds to lend you."
- "You still haven't repaid me the money I loaned to you the last time."
- "I have lost too many friends lending them money. I value relationships."

If you find it very hard to reject someone in person, try saying something like, "Please let me check my bank account and see if I can afford to lend you the money. I shall let you know again." You can follow up by sending the borrower a message or email to reply that you don't have the money the next day.

Now, what if the person continues to plead with you?

You don't have to feel obligated. And you certainly shouldn't ruin your own finances to bolster someone else's finances. It is perfectly fine for you to reject the request. Simply reply, "Sorry, I can't help you and I really don't wish to discuss further." However, you must be prepared to hang up the phone abruptly or walk away, depending on the situation. If that person brings up the subject again next time, just state firmly that if he or she keeps asking to borrow money, you shall end this conversation.

You need to formulate a policy of lending money now so that you are prepared to deal with a situation when someone comes to you to borrow money. This way, you won't be caught by surprise and are always ready to respond. Maybe you only lend in life and death situations. Or perhaps your policy is never to lend money to anyone under any circumstances. Whatever your money lending policy might be, it is important stick to it. Your response should be immediate and firm without any exceptions.

2. Helping in Other Ways

If your relatives and friends often need financial help, lending them cash will only address the symptom instead of providing the cure to the money disease. Whether it's careless spending or a lifestyle that's too big for them to handle, the underlying issue needs to be fixed rather than enabled.

You can offer help in other ways rather than providing a bailout. For example, if people ask for monetary assistance to help pay their credit card bills, you could propose to help them plan and set up a budget instead.

Never provide an easy way out of people's financial problems. Doing so is akin to kicking the can of money troubles down the road. It won't solve the underlying money issue. A better way would be to help them work through their financial stress.

3. Make the Loan in Writing

If you so decide that you really want to lend money to your relatives or friends, put the loan details in writing—even if they are your BBF (best friends forever). Having something in writing shows the borrower that you are serious about wanting your money back. The written note can also be a form of evidence in future if things turn ugly, for example, if your former BFF denies the loan even happened.

Be specific about repayment terms. Don't put in terms like "as soon as possible" because it is too vague to be meaningfully interpreted. What is "soon" to the lender may not mean the same for the borrower, because it can mean any time from the next day to never! Put in a specific date that you expect the debt to be fully repaid, and what happens should the borrower fails to meet the repayment dateline. Better still, spell out what will happen in the event you leave this world before the loan is repaid. Decide whether the debt would be forgiven or owed to your estate.

Not Lending Money Is Still the Best Policy

While the answer may be obvious to you by now, let me ask the question again: "Should you loan money to family and friends?" Really, this isn't an easy question to answer. Some may say, "Why not?" while others may insist, "Not to friends but family members and relatives are still alright." Loans between family members or friends often end up in unexpected problems. What's more, a survey conducted by one financial information site found that lending money to family members is the worst financial mistake!

One of the greatest disservices we can do to people is to lend them money when there is a likelihood they won't be able to pay back the full amount of the loan. Never lend money to people unless you're prepared to write off the loan. Because you likely would.

Are you willing to take a sibling, a relative, or a friend to court should they fail to pay you back the money owed to you? Only you can answer this question. Trust me, it's hard to make a decision to sue someone close to you. I know and I say this out of my own experience.

It was a day in the 1990s when my relative approached me to borrow $5,000. He was facing imminent retrenchment and was in financial distress after some money mismanagements. My relative promised to pay me back by installments of $150 per month. I wasn't rich by any standard at that time. Furthermore, I have little savings and had a mountain of debts to pay. However, I agreed to loan him the money out of my sympathy for his plight. Frankly, I had to use up almost all of my savings just to loan him the money. And I trusted him to pay me back by installments faithfully. But it didn't turn out that way. The payment stopped after just four rounds of installments. I called to remind him of the payment and was told he was cash-strapped. After many months of non-payment, I called my relative again but received the same answer. Another few months later, I called to remind him but he still couldn't afford to pay. I finally gave up and decided to forgive his debt. I was still poor then and had debts and bills to pay. I didn't make all these known to him though. What else can I possibly do? I didn't plan to bring my relative to court to recover my money because I still wish to keep the relationship alive.

Fast forward till today, my relative still didn't pay back what was owed to me though he has a stable job. We still meet each other during festive occasions, but he has never spoken about repaying the outstanding loan owed to me, not even once, but just acted as though nothing has ever happened. There is always a sense of awkwardness when we interact with each other nowadays. It's unfortunate and sad. Because the relationship is somewhat broken and is never the same again.

I had similar experience when I lend money to another two people—a friend and a business associate. In both cases, I didn't get my money back fully as well. I'm sure many others would have encountered similar cases too. Hence, the best policy is for us not to lend any money to anyone, even to those close to you, if you truly value relationships more than the money itself.

Although making mistakes is part and parcel of life, but when it concerns money, the fallout can be very costly. While some financial mistakes are minor, others can take many years to recover. What's worse is that often times, it's not just your finances that take a hit, but your relationships with others could suffer as well.

27

Tough Love Breeds Smart Children

Live so that when your children think of fairness, caring, and integrity, they think of you.
—H. Jackson Brown, Jr.

If you become wealthy one day, I encourage you to consider putting a notice somewhere in your house that reads: "Wealth given to people who didn't earn it can be detrimental to their health and future success!" Otherwise, at least hang up this notice in your mind. If you care for the future well-being of your children or loved ones, apply the same principle on this warning notice too.

Giving money to children is almost habitual for most parents. However, I have also frequently heard people saying that wealth doesn't last three generations. The wealth attrition rate is surprisingly high, affecting 90% of family fortunes according to one study conducted in the United States. Some of the cases have the money itself disappears, while in other cases, the family businesses go bust. Another study of first-generation millionaires, who gave significant wealth to their children, concluded that the second and third generations of children receiving the unearned money performed much worse financially when compared to their counterparts who never received any unearned financial resources.

The results of these studies show that when people are given a substantial amount of money they haven't earned, they won't have the perspective and judgment that are required to manage the riches wisely. And everything could be lost in due time.

Loving By Not Passing Down Unearned Wealth

While most children will inherit their parents' wealth one day, this might not be the case for all the children of ultra-successful people. Many business moguls are in fact planning to donate their fortunes to charity instead. They love their children so much that it means not passing down unearned wealth to them. Surprising, isn't it? For these parents who dote on their children and wish the very best for their children's future, surely there must be compelling reasons for doing so.

Let's examine the reasons of the following six billionaires who are examples of super-wealthy people choosing not to keep their massive wealth in the family:

1. Bill Gates

Bill and Melinda Gates are intending to give their three children "a minuscule portion" of their fortune, they told the *Daily Mail* in 2011. Bill Gates' net worth was around $121 billion as of January 2021. "It will mean they have to find their own way," Gates said. He believes it will compel his children to rely on themselves. "It's not a favor to kids to have them have huge sums of wealth. It distorts anything they might do, creating their own path." he told *This Morning* in 2016.

That is what the Gates are choosing to do—by not giving all their fortune to their children. They prefer to let their kids find their own directions in life, believing that to have everything taken care of for their children will only cloud their children's judgment in their journey of self-discovery. The Gates truly desire to have their children be the best they can be.

The couple plans to put the majority of their fortune toward charitable causes, namely the Bill & Melinda Gates Foundation, which aims to eradicate disease, poverty and hunger across the globe. Along with fellow billionaire Warren Buffett, Bill and Melinda Gates also helped create the Giving Pledge in 2010, which encourages more of the super-rich to leave the majority of their wealth to philanthropic causes.

2. Warren Buffett

Billionaire investor, Warren Buffett, told *Fortune* in 1986 that he wants to leave his kids enough money so that they would feel they could do anything, but not so much that they could do nothing. *The Washington Post* reported in 2014 that Buffett plans to leave his three children $2 billion each. That's considered a very huge sum of money though, but it's still nowhere near the full scope of his $88 billion fortune as of January 2021. The rest of it will go toward philanthropic causes.

As a co-founder of the Giving Pledge along with friend and fellow billionaire Bill Gates, Buffett is committed to donating more that 99% of his wealth to charity during his lifetime or at the time of his death.

3. Mark Zuckerberg

When Facebook CEO Mark Zuckerberg's daughter, Max, was born in 2015, his wife (Priscilla Chan) and him made an interesting announcement that they don't plan to leave their child their billions fortune. Instead, the couple founded the Chan Zuckerberg Initiative, a limited liability company dedicated to personalized learning, curing disease, connecting people and building strong communities around the world.

On December 2, 2015, the couple wrote a letter to Max that was posted in Zuckerberg's Facebook page: "We will give 99% of our Facebook shares—currently about $45 billion—during our lives to advance this mission. We know this is a small contribution compared to all the resources and talents of those already working on these issues. But we want to do what we can, working alongside many others." Zuckerberg was worth an estimated $97 billion as of January 2021.

4. Michael Bloomberg

Rather than leaving the entirety of his fortune (about $55 billion as of January 2021) to his daughters directly, former New York City mayor, Michael Bloomberg, plans to invest in philanthropic organizations that will help create a better future for them.

In his Giving Pledge letter, Bloomberg writes: "If you want to do something for your children and show how much you love them, the single best thing—by far—is to support organizations that will create a better world for them and their children. And by giving, we inspire others to give of themselves, whether their money or their time."

5. Andrew Lloyd Webber

Composer Andrew Lloyd Webber, best known for musicals such as *Phantom of the Opera* and *Cats*, is reportedly worth over $1 billion. However, his 5 children won't be getting rich off their dad's success. Webber told *Mirror* in 2008, "I don't believe in inherited money at all. I am not in favor of children suddenly finding a lot of money coming their way because then they have no incentive to work. So, I will give them a start in life but they ain't going to end up owning my company." Rather, Webber hopes his earnings will be put back into theater and go toward helping upcoming musicians.

6. Chuck Feeney

Chuck Feeney is the most generous billionaire you probably never heard of. Feeney, the co-founder of Duty Free Shoppers Group, made his money selling luxury duty free goods to travelers across the world. He's a billionaire who is trying to go broke within his own lifetime by giving all his money away. Once worth about $8 billion, Feeney is technically no longer a billionaire after donating his entire fortune to charitable causes. He signed over everything to Atlantic Philanthropies, the foundation he founded in 1982. He has left himself with about $2 million to live on— less than 0.001% of the $8 billion he has given away.

Feeney rejects the trappings of wealth himself. He doesn't own a home or a car, and famously wears a watch that was bought for just $15.

Warren Buffett has this to say about Feeney: "Chuck has set an example... he is my hero and Bill Gates' hero. He should be everybody's hero."

Although his children won't be seeing a dime of their inheritance, they understood their father's goodwill. One of his daughters, Leslie Feeney Baily, told *The New York Times* in 2007, "It is eccentric, but he sheltered us from people using the money to treat us differently. It made us normal people."

Tough Love

Can you see a consistent pattern in the mindset of the mega-rich from the above examples? I'm sure they love their children very much, as much as we love our own children. However, these highly successful people love and care enough not to pass excessive wealth down to their children for their sake. That's called tough love. We are frequently forced to be cruel in order to be kind. It's tough, and that's why it's love. Showing our children tough love today will undoubtedly save them troubles and heartaches tomorrow.

Children brought up by parents practicing tough love are more likely to become well-rounded personalities with well-developed characters. The wealthy understand that leaving significant inheritances or giving unearned wealth to their offspring would be detrimental to their children's future success.

If you want your children to develop self-control, empathy, determination and discipline, the tough love approach is best. Giving money freely to your children is easy, exercising tough love by restricting your children's finances isn't. Teach them how to fish instead of providing the fish. If your children are capable, they will be able to make money and build wealth themselves when they grow up. Otherwise, they will just be wasting your money no matter how much you give them. So, do your children this great favor by giving them tough love for their own good.

Prepare Your Children to Live a Responsible Adult Life

Your children are impressionable. You can mold them into prudent and responsible financial stewards or you can leave them alone, hoping that one day they will grow up to be wise with their money. Unfortunately, the chances of your children being money-savvy are very slim without any guidance. Remember, financial literacy is never taught in your children's schools, colleges or universities.

In my opinion, my parents shouldn't be obligated to leave their money for me upon their passing. That's because it's their money, not mine. And my parents certainly can do whatever they want with their money. I don't think my parents owe me anything financially after I gain independence from them as an adult. My parents raised me to be who I am today, and words can never explain how thankful and grateful I am for them.

Similarly, I don't believe I owe my adult children anything financially. I surely wouldn't want my children to feel entitled to financial support that comes too easily. Such sense of entitlement would almost certainly wreck their financial future. Once my children are grown up to be independent adults earning their own income, I won't feel obligated to be financially accountable and responsible for their lives. That's where parental guidance becomes crucial to prepare the children to live their future adult life in a responsible way.

TOUGH LOVE BREEDS SMART CHILDREN

Just as I don't want my financial life intertwined with my parents, I don't want my financial life intertwined with my adult children as well. This isn't to suggest that I wouldn't help my children in any way if they needed something. Rather, it's simply a case of not wanting them to develop a sense of entitlement or a crutch mentality.

28

Enough Is Enough

It's good to have money and the things that money can buy, but it's good, too, to check up once in a while and make sure that you haven't lost the things that money can't buy.
—George Lorimer

How much money do we need to be happy? This is a timeless question. But we really don't need nearly as much money as most people think. Many studies confirmed that anyone can be happy at a basic standard of living, and an elevated level of living doesn't mean people can get much more happiness. More money can contribute to more happiness only to a certain point. Makes sense, doesn't it? I mean, do you honestly believe that people living in the past were not as happy before the invention of microwave ovens, or the arrival of smartphones?

Sure, there are some basic things we need to be happy. Things like: a roof over our heads, a sense of purpose, a few close friends, healthy relationships with our loved ones, good health, etc. Other than the roof over your head, most of the things that will make you happy don't cost you money. However, very few of us get this. Many would continue their pursuit of chasing after more, some more, and even more. It is a never-ending pursuit after more things. In the end, people will come to a realization that having more won't make them happier.

The Fisherman and the Businessman

Here's a wonderful short story, written by Brazilian author Paolo Coelho, about an encounter between fisherman and a businessman:

There was once a businessman who was sitting by the beach in a small Brazilian village.

As he sat, he saw a Brazilian fisherman rowing a small boat towards the shore having caught quite few big fish.

The businessman was impressed and asked the fisherman, "How long does it take you to catch so many fish?"

The fisherman replied, "Oh, just a short while."

"Then why don't you stay longer at sea and catch even more?" The businessman was astonished.

"This is enough to feed my whole family," the fisherman said.

The businessman then asked, "So, what do you do for the rest of the day?"

The fisherman replied, "Well, I usually wake up early in the morning, go out to sea and catch a few fish, then go back and play with my kids. In the afternoon, I take a nap with my wife, and evening comes, I join my buddies in the village for a drink— we play guitar, sing and dance throughout the night."

The businessman offered a suggestion to the fisherman.

"I graduated with a PhD in business management. And I could help you to become a more successful person. From now on, you should spend more time at sea and try to catch as many fish as possible. When you have saved enough money, you could buy a bigger boat and catch even more fish. Soon you will be able to afford to buy more boats, set up your own company, your own production plant for canned food and distribution network. By then, you will have moved out of this village and to Sao Paulo, where you can set up HQ to manage your other branches."

The fisherman continues, "And after that?"

The businessman laughs heartily, "After that, you can live like a king in your own house, and when the time is right, you can go public and float your shares in the Stock Exchange, and you will be rich."

The fisherman asks, "And after that?"

The businessman says, "After that, you can finally retire, you can move to a house by the fishing village, wake up early in the morning, catch a few fish, then return home to play with kids, have a nice afternoon nap with your wife, and when evening comes, you can join your buddies for a drink, play the guitar, sing and dance throughout the night!"

The fisherman was puzzled, "Isn't that what I am doing now?"

We don't need a lot of money to be happy. For most of us, we already have enough resources to be happy. It's just that some people make financial blunders to go into debt to buy things they think would make them happier. But they soon realize that such happiness is temporal, and their debts would soon weigh them down. The story of the fisherman and the businessman is a perfect illustration of how little we need in order to be happy.

The Little Things That Bring Happiness

The important things in life that bring basic joy to people are virtually free. The route to happiness isn't necessarily through major events like getting married, moving house, being on a vacation, receiving keys of new car, or even getting that all-important job promotion. Very often, it's the little things making us smile each day that give us true happiness.

The following are some examples of the things in daily life that make people happy:

- Waking up to a beautiful and sunny day
- Hugging and kissing your spouse before starting your day
- Giving your spouse a goodnight kiss
- Eating breakfast in bed with your spouse
- Watching the sunrise or sunset
- Watching the rain outside in the comfort of your cozy house
- Enjoying the smell of freshness outside early in the morning
- Smiling at a stranger you see in public
- A stranger giving you a genuine smile
- A hug from somebody you care about
- A gesture of support or kindness from family and friends

- Window shopping with family and friends
- Chatting with a friend you haven't met for a long time
- Soaking in the bathtub after a hard day's work
- Spending some time alone after a busy day
- Spending time with your children
- Playing with your pets
- Laughing out loud at a funny memory
- Your children helping with housework
- Helping your spouse prepare and cook a family meal
- Trying out a new recipe and creating something delicious
- Holding hands with someone you love
- Playing games with family or friends
- Watching your favorite movies or shows
- Reading your favorite books or magazines
- Listening to songs or music you love
- Playing the piano, violin, guitar or other musical instruments
- Singing karaoke songs with your spouse
- Receiving gifts from someone who cares about you
- Helping people solve their problems

The list above is limitless. You can add on to this list as many things as you wish. Happiness doesn't cost you much. In fact, many things that you can enjoy anytime are free. Simple pleasures in life can help us build meaningful lives—both for ourselves and others.

Decide When to Stop

Work-life balance can seem like an impossible feat nowadays. People's fear of losing their jobs lead them to work longer hours. Today's advancement in technology also causes people to work more, as they become connected online and accessible round-the-clock. It is not uncommon to witness people staying back to work way passed the official working hours. Many continue to response to calls, emails and messages even when vacationing because their internet-connected gadgets never leave them wherever they go. Such long hours of work will definitely affect their quality of life.

Harvard Business School conducted a survey and found a whopping 94% of professionals working more than 50 hours per week; and nearly 50% said they worked more than 65 hours per week. The compounding stress from the inhumanely long hours of work, lack of rest, and poor work-life balance is certainly damaging. It affects the quality of life and could even hurt relationships, health, and the overall well-being of a person.

While money does buy some happiness, it isn't the only element. Along with healthy relationship, good health conditions, purposeful work, and spiritual wellbeing, money is just one piece of the jigsaw puzzle in the overall satisfaction of your life. How much money is enough for you? After you make your first million dollars, you may want to pursue the next million. And if you become a multimillionaire, you may go on a quest to become a billionaire When will you stop chasing after more money?

The choice is entirely yours to make. You need to decide whether it is worth your time and effort to chase after more wealth. By the way, most millionaires could have lived similar lifestyles as the billionaires. The only difference between the millionaire and the billionaire is the number of zeros in their net worth statements. Other than that, many of the things own by billionaires are things the millionaires can also afford to buy.

When you have done well in building wealth to a respectable level, the time will come when you decide that enough is enough. A time when you desire to enjoy life, spend more quality time with your loved ones, go holidaying around the world, or simply get your work-life balance to tip more towards life. There is really no point killing yourself just to have more riches.

Negative Consequences of Wealth

We need to be aware that there are negative consequences of wealth too. Rich people can develop arrogance, pride, lack of empathy, and may even suffer isolation. Many tend to take things or people for granted after acquiring substantial riches. Money, if not handled carefully, can make us materialistic and conceited.

It can also lead us to miss out on life's simple pleasures, and not fully appreciate the gifts of nature, family or friends.

One of the greatest regrets at the end of people's life is not being able to spend more quality time with their loved ones. Consider the opportunity costs in the process of accumulating more wealth. Be mindful of the amount of time taken out of us to amass more wealth, and the opportunities we forego as a result.

You Can't Take Wealth with You

You can't take your possessions to the grave. It's a fact of life. No one is born into this world with an underwear attached. You were born into the world with nothing, and you shall leave this world with nothing. When it is time for you to go, you go alone. There is absolutely nothing in this world that you can bring along with you. Don't take your possessions as your main priority in life. Besides, there are other aspects of life as well as people around you that are much more valuable.

As reported by *The Daily Telegraph*, a survey of 2,198 people who had lost a relative found that 83% had been given advice concerning:

- Relationships (62%)
- Careers (56%)
- Family (43%)
- Education (39%)
- Finances (32%)
- Happiness (29%)
- Putting right past mistakes (21%)
- Living life without regrets (17%)
- Taught a lesson (6%)

The last words of the dying to their loved ones are most often advice about relationships, where it tops the poll at 62%. For many people, choosing to build relationships over building wealth can be challenging. The reason may be because the accumulation of money is easier to measure as compared to relationships. However, we must be aware that most of the things in life that truly make us happy aren't easily quantifiable. They are much harder to count as compared to money. Finances, careers and possessions are all part of life's rich tapestry. But sooner or later, we will recognize that relationships and friendships are the things that would matter to us most.

No matter how wealthy we are, we can't take anything with us when we leave this world. While on our deathbed, I'm sure the last thing on our mind is wishing to have one final look at our bank account!

Conclusion

The principles of wealth building have not changed much for centuries. Many people around the world are looking for the secret to becoming wealthy. After spending many years of my time searching for the secret to riches, I realize that the only secret to building wealth is by understanding the wealth principles, and most importantly, live by them. These are the rules of wealth that have stood the test of time. The way we handle our money inevitably affects our financial future.

Wealth gives you freedom and choices. If you don't have money, you won't have much freedom. And the choices available to you may not be the ones you truly desire. This means that if you have limited cash, you are left without a choice most of the time. You obviously need some money to cover all your basic expenses in order to survive in this world. Beyond that, how much money you need will be determined by what kind of life you want to live.

While money is undeniably an important aspect in our lives, it isn't everything. Your relationships with others around you matter too. If your vision is blurred because all you see is money, it will be difficult for you to cherish life and be reminded of the good times with your family and friends. The only thing between you and the people in your life is your relationship with them. Many people end up with broken relationships in their quest for wealth above everything else. Never follow their footsteps or you will regret later in life. I see many people slogging away in the name of money. Some of them are suffering from poor health as a result. What good is wealth without health? Don't be one of them. It's really not worth for you to chase after money at any cost. You must exercise complete control over your money, and not let money control you.

Live a fulfilling life by blessing others with your time and riches. A hoarded blessing is never enjoyed as richly as a shared one. Let me conclude by sharing *The Paradox of Our Age* essay written by Dr. Bob Moorehead, a retired former pastor of Seattle's Overlake Christian Church. This meaningful essay was published in 1995 in his book *Words Aptly Spoken*—a collection of prayers, homilies, and monologues used in his sermons and radio broadcasts.

The Paradox of Our Age

We have taller buildings but shorter tempers; wider freeways but narrower viewpoints; we spend more but have less; we buy more but enjoy it less; we have bigger houses and smaller families; more conveniences, yet less time; we have more degrees but less sense; more knowledge but less judgment; more experts, yet more problems; we have more gadgets but less satisfaction; more medicine, yet less wellness; we take more vitamins but see fewer results. We drink too much; smoke too much; spend too recklessly; laugh too little; drive too fast; get too angry quickly; stay up too late; get up too tired; read too seldom; watch TV too much and pray too seldom.

We have multiplied our possessions, but reduced our values; we fly in faster planes to arrive there quicker, to do less and return sooner; we sign more contracts only to realize fewer profits; we talk too much; love too seldom and lie too often. We've learned how to make a living, but not a life; we've added years to life, not life to years. We've been all the way to the moon and back, but have trouble crossing the street to meet the new neighbor. We've conquered outer space, but not inner space; we've done larger things, but not better things; we've cleaned up the air,

CONCLUSION

but polluted the soul; we've split the atom, but not our prejudice; we write more, but learn less; plan more, but accomplish less; we make faster planes, but longer lines; we learned to rush, but not to wait; we have more weapons, but less peace; higher incomes, but lower morals; more parties, but less fun; more food, but less appeasement; more acquaintances, but fewer friends; more effort, but less success. We build more computers to hold more information, to produce more copies than ever, but have less communication; drive smaller cars that have bigger problems; build larger factories that produce less. We've become long on quantity, but short on quality.

These are the times of fast foods and slow digestion; tall men, but short character; steep in profits, but shallow relationships. These are times of world peace, but domestic warfare; more leisure and less fun; higher postage, but slower mail; more kinds of food, but less nutrition. These are days of two incomes, but more divorces; these are times of fancier houses, but broken homes. These are days of quick trips, disposable diapers, cartridge living, throw-away morality, one-night stands, overweight bodies and pills that do everything from cheer, to prevent, quiet or kill. It is a time when there is much in the show window and nothing in the stock room. Indeed, these are the times!

—Dr. Bob Moorehead

You have come to the end of this book and I surely hope it has played a part in your learning, growing and becoming. If you're still with me up to this point, I would say you're truly amazing. You're unlike most people who may have bought many books, but never get to finish reading most of them. However, you must take note that nobody has ever become wealthy just by reading books; it's only by applying the knowledge you've gained that you can create wealth. Rest assured that you'll be greatly enriched if you master your money to become a better steward of your finances.

Begin your wealth journey now. Here's wishing you greater prosperity and happiness!

ALSO BY KELVIN WONG

BOOK DESCRIPTION

All parents share a common hope that their children will have a lifetime of happiness and success. Unfortunately, we only have our kids for a brief moment. We can only hope our gifts to our children will be sufficient for their well-being even when we can't be with them anymore. The truth is, the greatest gift you can give to your children isn't money or possessions. It's wisdom. This book was born out of the author's desire to leave a tangible account of his experience—taught by the school of hard knocks—to guide his sons to live with greater purpose and significance. It contains timeless and valuable lessons applicable to everyone, young and old alike. Indeed, wisdom is the greatest gift for your children's success, and yours too!

In *The Greatest Gift to My Children*, you'll learn how to:
- Discover your life purpose and live your passion
- Dream big and believe in yourself
- Visualize your success and turn your dream into reality
- Overcome fears, uncertainties and self-doubts
- Improve your financial health
- Stop chasing money and have it chasing you instead
- Live a truly happy, successful and fulfilled life

ABOUT THE AUTHOR

Kelvin Wong is a millionaire investor and landlord. He held senior management positions in multinational corporations before leaving corporate life in 2007 to focus on managing his own investments. At the age of 39, Kelvin reached financial independence, and has retired with a multimillion-dollar property portfolio in Singapore, Australia and Malaysia. A Dean's List graduate, he holds a Bachelor of Business degree in Marketing and Management Science from Edith Cowan University. When he is not writing, Kelvin spends most of his time reading, cycling, swimming, playing tennis, working out in the gym, and researching stocks and properties to buy. Visit his website at www.KelvinWong.com for more information.

CONNECT WITH KELVIN WONG

Thanks for reading my book. I really appreciate it and trust that you have benefitted from the book in many ways. Here are my social media coordinates...

Facebook - https://www.facebook.com/AuthorKelvinWong
LinkedIn - https://www.linkedin.com/in/kelvinwongkc
Twitter - https://twitter.com/kelvinwongkc
Website - https://www.KelvinWong.com

www.ingramcontent.com/pod-product-compliance
Lightning Source LLC
Chambersburg PA
CBHW021401210526
45463CB00001B/179